GROWING UP AND

LIKING IT

~ More Steps to a Happier Self ~

By Dolores Ayotte

Endorsements

"Growing Up and Liking It" (The Donut Holes) is the second in a series of books written by Dolores Ayotte. I truly enjoyed it, much like her first book, "I'm Not Perfect and It's Okay" because it seemed to fill in the gaps. "Growing Up and Liking It" takes you on an adventure filled with humorous quips and anecdotes about life's experiences. The simple tips shared by Dolores help the readers to find meaning in their own lives in order to better cope with their own personal challenges. It is once again, a hand's on recipe. The recommended tips help individuals to be the best they can be no matter the circumstances.

Lorraine Gauthier B.A. (Psychology) Sun Life Advisor

A most inspiring and enjoyable sequel to, "I'm Not Perfect and It's Okay". Once again, the author enlightens the reader with her wisdom and natural ability to express and teach others from her own life experiences. As a result, this book gives you insight on simple life strategies to a happier self. I loved it!

Gloria Korell

Dolores's second book was as much joy to read as her first. It's full of insight and wisdom. I wrote her when I was done reading her manuscript and told Dolores how hard it was to put down "Growing Up and Liking It" (The Donut Holes) once I started to read it. It's one book that totally had me hooked from start to finish.

Linda Briscoe

Living happier and more fulfilling lives is ever more daunting in these stressful times when finding a balance between work, home, recreation and relationships often seems out of reach. How refreshing it is then to read Dolores Ayotte's latest book "Growing Up and Liking It (The Donut Holes)" and to discover simple, effective steps for finding a balanced approach to happier living. This wife, parent, grandmother, gardener, storyteller, teacher and author shares her wonderful philosophy for living a happy, rewarding life using her easy to follow "nuggets" of wisdom. Her unique writing style borrows from the quips and quotations of many of the world's wise and quotable persons passed down through the ages, which she blends with her own life experiences to guide the reader to better life coping skills. This is a book to be read as one would eat a box of "donut holes" from the local Donut and Coffee Shop, one bite at a time so as to savor the flavor and to digest the lessons taught from your favorite ones.

Gilbert Frontain - Director Human Resources (Retired)

For Fred, our children, and
our grandchildren...*with love*.

Acknowledgments

I would like to thank my husband Fred for all his support and guidance in the writing of my books. I could not have done it without him. I would also like to thank our three daughters, Cheryl, Andrea, Joanna, and all our grandchildren for being such an inspiration to me. Once again, I would like to gratefully acknowledge Andrea for her influence in spurring me on to revisit this dream of mine and for writing the foreword for *Growing Up and Liking It*.

Thank you to Lorraine Gauthier, Gloria Korell, Linda Briscoe, and Gil Frontain for reading my manuscript and endorsing it. I am grateful to my friends, family, and acquaintances that have shown so much encouragement and support. I am very much honored that you have taken the time to purchase, read, and share my first book *I'm Not Perfect and It's Okay* with your family and friends.

Some of you have gone the extra mile to promote my books. Those who particularly stand out are Shirley Sarafinchan, Lorraine Gauthier, and Gloria Korell. Thank you for reaching out to your friends, extended family, fellow employees, and bookstores/gift shops on my behalf. I very much appreciate this extra effort. I would like to further acknowledge Andrea, Shirley, and Lorraine and thank them for hosting a book launch for me in my hometown of Winnipeg, Manitoba. I would like to say a very special thank you to my brother-in-law Barry Merrell, my daughter Andrea Cockerill, and my dear husband Fred for the fine job they did of proofreading my manuscript.

I would also like to thank a few of my southern friends, Jan Olson, Alice Bakke, and Kay Wielinski for their wonderful support and effort to sell books on my behalf as well as for hosting a book signing for me in Mesa, Arizona. A special thank you to Jan Olson for making and providing the friendship necklaces to accompany the books sold at the Arts and Crafts Fair in Mesa, Arizona and to Jan, Alice, and Kay for spending the day with me at my book table on more than one occasion. You have all been such an inspiration to me.

Last, but not least, I would like thank each and every one of you for reading *Growing Up and Liking It*. Not unlike *I'm Not Perfect and It's Okay*, this book has also been written in recipe form for all those who can relate to it or learn from it. At last, this part of my dream has been realized because I feel that this second book encompasses the final thirteen steps of my recommendations for a happier self.

Table of Contents

Foreword

I have always known that my mother could give sound advice if the occasion arose. I have gone to her often throughout my years at university, during my employment as a social worker, and now in my years of mothering. Sometimes as children in the process of growing up, we can't always see our mothers as women, as if the role of mother negates being a woman. As I have gotten older, I have taken a step back, and I have learned to look at my mother through the eyes of a woman looking at another woman. As an adult, I see a woman who passionately cares about people, not just her own children but all people who may have suffered or who are suffering. She knows suffering, but she also knows the power of hope, knowledge, and self-love. These are such simple concepts, yet many times they are so hard to grasp in times of despair. I have had my own times of despair, from a firstborn being in the NICU to the heartbreak of some of the tougher times during the mothering of my own children. It is during those times that I have called my mother knowing I would receive the words of guidance that I so longed to hear. Her guidance is not complicated but rather straightforward and practical. Her words are just the remedy needed in times when complications and stress seem to dominate our lives.

My mother is educated, but it is more through her own painful trials that she has learned life's most valuable lessons. I feel that it is because of her compassionate heart that she writes this book full of wisdom and raw knowingness. She initially wrote her books so that her children and grandchildren could benefit from her life experience. Her goal was to spare them the suffering from falling as hard and as deep as she did during her most painful times. It is with this compassion that she shares her recipe for a more balanced life with her readers.

My mother writes in much the same way as she would talk to you if you came to her for advice. Her words are well thought out, gentle, and non-judgmental. You can feel this positive energy throughout the pages of her book. Two of the greatest gifts my mother has ever given me are: to believe in something bigger than myself, and to honor the beliefs of my neighbor. It is because of these wonderful gifts that I now see the world in color instead of black and white. What joy it has been to live life with such an open heart. Although I am her daughter, I no longer ignore the woman my mother is nor the woman my mother wants me to be. In doing so, my eyes are now wide open and able to see the gentle wisdom that was always there right in front of me. I am ever so grateful that now you too can share in my mother's wisdom and grace. In doing so may your heart be open to the gifts her book has to offer. Enjoy!

Andrea Cockerill – BA (Psychology), BSW

Introduction

I am back to write the second half of my suggestions for a happier self. The first half found in *I'm Not Perfect and It's Okay* consisted of thirteen steps. I considered this to be the bulk of my suggestions. The tips in this book are what I am going to refer to as the "donut holes," and they will finish off the theme of the first book. At this point, I think that these chapters will be shorter, not unlike the center of the donuts being smaller than the donut itself, but tasty just the same. Hopefully, these will be just as good as the original baker's dozen and, although not as long, equally easy to comprehend and digest.

Once again, I must admit that I never considered myself to be an author when I first started to put pen to paper. My need to write far outweighed my literary expertise. I will also admit that as time goes by, I see myself as much more of a philosopher than an author in the sense that I do a lot of thinking and analyzing before I attempt to write anything down. I have been mulling over these thoughts, not only for a number of months, but literally for a number of years. As the years go by, however, my passion for writing and the desire for my voice to be heard increases. Perhaps like the honing of any other skill, I now classify myself as a motivational author.

My writing is meant for others who think like me or who can relate to some of the experiences I am about to share with you. Plain and simple, this is what I consider to be a heart book. It's written from my heart to any and all hearts that are open to its message.

My previous book has been a series of essays that have brought me great joy in the writing of them. I agree with Charles Poore in saying that, "An essayist is a lucky person who has found a way to discourse without being interrupted."[1] I believe I am one of these lucky people who have been given both the inspiration and the opportunity. If you have not read my first book, I would encourage you to do so. If you already have and are reading this book, I thank you from the bottom of my heart for allowing me to share my "bits of wisdom" with you yet again.

Many times in life people offer advice without the benefit of the voice of experience. The suggestions that I offered in my first book as well as the tips I am about to offer in *Growing Up and Liking It* are based on personal experience. I know that they work because I have lived them. When I struggle in life, it is most often as a result of losing sight of my own recommendations. It is at this time that I find it necessary to remind myself of the steps I have suggested for the benefit of all, including myself. When this occurs, I usually do a reality check to ensure that I am practicing what I teach. I have chosen to use the word *teach* instead of *preach* out of personal preference for "it's easier to preach ten sermons than it is to live one."[2] If and when you really want to improve your life, the steps provided are a sure proof method to a more enjoyable life. These steps are not about removing your woes but rather about providing ideas for a better coping mechanism that may improve your ability to face what life has to offer. Always try to remember that "the Will of God will never take you where the Grace of God will not protect you."[3] I have really learned to grow up over the last several years, and it has been beneficial to all, especially me and those closest to me. This is the reason why I think the title to my book is so appropriate. As I enter into my twilight years, I want to permanently shed my insecurities and enter this final stage of life with as much grace and wisdom as humanly possible. I have been an observant student for the majority of my life. Perhaps now, after all these years, I can get into the driver's seat and call myself a good teacher. I have succeeded in learning to "teach without classroom walls" and I have now written my own motivational books to go along with this philosophy. This experience has been extremely liberating for me. I hope by reading what I have to say and by incorporating some of my suggestions into your life, that you too can find a sense of true freedom and peace.

Shake It Off

What better way to start off this book than with the telling of a story? Some things never change! The story I am about to tell you is actually one of the reasons I am writing this second book. After writing thirteen chapters, I wasn't sure if I had thirteen more points to offer. I knew that I had more to say/write, so I'm starting off not knowing just how far this book will go. I am optimistic nonetheless because once I started to write my first book I never ceased to amaze even myself as the ideas continued to flow one after the other. Once again, I cannot take full credit for these ideas as I remind myself that, at times, they seem to come to me from a well much deeper than my own. In advance, I already know that I will be drawing from this same resource. This was the inspiration for my first book, which was based on my own, personal relationship with God. I am forever grateful for this "gift" of insight, which has been bestowed upon me and many others before me. I have learned that "the task ahead of us is never as great as the power behind us."[4] This has been demonstrated by the wealth of quotes, bits of expertise, and words of wisdom that I have been able to share with you as I tell my story. "Honesty is the first chapter in the book of wisdom."[5] Due to the fact that honesty is one of the characteristics that I most highly regard, I have made every effort to relate all my stories as honestly and as accurately as possible. I know that honesty and wisdom go hand and hand. Wisdom is another trait I hold in high esteem, and I will continue to incorporate the "little bits" of it that I have observed or used along the way as I share my ideas with you.

Several years ago when my husband was enjoying a hockey game at our local arena, not unlike many of the other spectators at the event, he needed a washroom break. I don't know if your arena is like ours, but most sport venues never seem to have enough bathrooms. There are always long lines. It isn't so bad if you use the facilities during the game; however, if you need to use them during intermission, you can be sure that the people will be lined up. Sometimes the queue is right out the door. Obviously, because this event occurred in the male washroom, I am only repeating this story as told to me by my husband when he got home from the hockey game. He still had laughter in his voice as he tried to describe it to me.

Often times, you can try to retell a story but for some reason or another, it doesn't always have the same funny effect. I must say that this was the exception because I found this story every bit as cute and as funny as my husband did. As he was waiting in line, he noticed a father in the washroom with his young son. The father was trying to force the boy to hurry up as he was using the facilities due to the long line up of other men waiting for their turns. The young boy just looked up at his dad and said that he wasn't finished. He added that he needed time to "shake it off." My husband went on to say that the whole room cracked up with laughter over what the little boy had said because all of them could relate to it. That little boy wasn't going anywhere until he had finished what he had started. He was taking care of business in the way that his father had taught him on many earlier occasions. It was the only way he knew how to do what he needed to get done. "In every child who is born, under no matter what circumstances, and of no matter what parents, the potentiality of the human race is born again."[6] So simple was this basic act, taught to this young boy, at such an early stage of life.

How powerful our role is as parents and educators. No matter how many other men were in the room, that young son knew that his dad had taught him how to do things right. Therefore, it was exactly what he intended to do. He had no idea what everyone found so amusing. He was only finishing what he had started because he had complete and total trust in what his dad had taught him. There was no question about it! In fact, he had so much faith in what his father had taught him that he took the opportunity to remind him of it. "Small opportunities are often the beginning of great enterprises."[7] The lessons were twofold in the sense that the lad was doing as he had been instructed, and the dad was learning just how powerful he was in the teaching of one of life's simple lessons. These simple, little everyday lessons are the first stepping stones for all the lessons to follow. That young boy, at least at this impressionable age, was learning to emulate his father in all that he did or had been taught to do. Yes, he wasn't quite finished yet.

Therefore, I too must learn from one of my life lessons. Although these chapters may be shorter, I still must finish what I started. I feel it is necessary to write this second one in order to tie up the loose ends after the first book. For all I know, there could even be a third! It is the only way that I know how to get the job done.

My daughter, who had first shown an interest in my notebook of special quotes and notes, amused me the other day when she agreed that she couldn't see a book in them. She made me chuckle when she said, "It really was about reading between the lines." How true! I've noticed that since my husband has also read my book, I'm starting to hear more and more of my own philosophy on life with the odd quote thrown in. I'm starting to wonder if this is my biggest dream come true or my worst nightmare. We really are on a level playing field. My family now has access to all my little quotes and quips right at their fingertips ready to regurgitate them as the need arises. They now know me inside and out, and my life is fast becoming like an open book. Not to worry, however, because I have been enjoying this information for years. No sooner will they make use of one of my famous quotes when dealing with me, I will come up with a new one, not unlike the missing baby tooth that has been replaced by a permanent one. Such fun, this verbal sparring has become. It really does keep one mentally alert! "The quality of a person's life is in direct proportion to their commitment to excellence, regardless of their chosen field of endeavour."[8] So once again, I stress that it is not so much about what you do but more about how you do it that counts. This could get both interesting and challenging as I try to keep one step ahead of the game as I finish what I have started. It seems that I am sticking my neck even farther out on a limb with my views but I believe it is a risk worth taking.

In most instances, discussing our views and opinions is a good thing. I agree with Bernard Edmonds when he says, "To dream anything that you want to dream, that is the beauty of the human mind. To do anything that you want to do, that is the strength of the human will. To trust yourself to test your limits, that is the courage to succeed."[9] With that thought in mind, I have now completed the essence of the first chapter of my second book. I have every intention of finishing what I have started as I search for the excellence that I feel we are all capable of, no matter what our walk in life may be, as long as we have the desire to succeed. "The difference between a successful person and others is not a lack of strength, not a lack of knowledge, but rather a lack of will."[10] Not unlike that little boy, I too have been taught to finish the job. I have both the desire and the need to do it right, even if it is only according to my own experiences and expectations of myself. Once again, my desire is to share what those experiences have taught me along the way. Some of these findings may also be of benefit to you. I sincerely hope so!

Step 1 ~ It does not matter when you started a special project or had a big dream. What matters is being open to fulfilling that dream when the time is right. Don't stop until you have had the opportunity to "shake it off." When the job is complete, you'll know. It's a great idea to set aside some personal time as often as possible to do a little soul searching in order to fully benefit from all my suggestions. These are just a few examples of some questions that you can ask yourself to better implement the first step. What goals have you set for yourself? Have you written them down? Create a dream board and clip out pictures or quotes that remind you of your goals every day. Place your board in an area where you'll see it and be inspired by it daily.

Open the Door

Did you ever notice that as you open the door to let in the sunlight, the more you see the dust on the floor or the surfaces around you? Did you know that the more you open the door to God's light, the more you also notice the dust that exists inside you? This dust lives inside each and every one of us. A lot of people don't like to do housekeeping. Therefore, they prefer to keep it dark inside so that they don't have to clean up their act. Are you one of those people? Initially it is a huge decision to do some major housekeeping, whether speaking figuratively or literally, but once the dust settles and you can clearly see what needs to be done, it becomes easier. In my opinion, we have two choices here. "This one step—choosing a goal and sticking to it—changes everything."[11] We can choose to keep ourselves in the dark and keep sweeping all the dust under the carpet. We don't ever really need to face or deal with any of life's difficult moments or situations. All we need to do is sweep, sweep, and sweep. The carpet of our life may have a few bumps in it, but that's no big deal. We know where the bumps are, and we will just walk over or around them rather than lift the carpet to clean them up.

Although, it's important to remember that "the starting point of all achievement is desire. Keep this constantly in mind. Weak desires bring weak results, just as a small amount of fire makes a small amount of heat."[12] Plenty of people choose to live their lives this way. They have little or no desire to change their circumstances. It's their choice. We live in a free world. We all have free will, freedom of choice, freedom of expression, and several other freedoms that are too numerous to mention. In a way, at first blush, this choice of ignoring the dust or covering it up seems like the easier choice rather than actually opening the door, seeing the dust, and then doing something about it. A lot of us are tempted to go this route because it is the route of least resistance and therefore appears to be less work. We also have another choice. I feel the need, nevertheless, to ask another question here to better make my point. Have you ever noticed, whether at home when it comes to doing chores or at work when it comes to job demands, that the less you do or accomplish on a daily basis the more overwhelming it eventually becomes? In my opinion, the more you keep things up by doing a little along the way, the less exhausting and overwhelming the task will be later on. "Better keep yourself clean and bright: You are the window through which you must see the world."[13] No matter how you slice it, you will eventually have to houseclean one way or the other. If you try to clean up your act along the way, you will have the benefits that go with it. The reward, for living life this way, far exceeds the energy it takes to get the work done. "You cannot escape the responsibility of tomorrow by evading it today."[14]

I want to share one of my most profound findings with you. Did you know that the door to your heart and soul opens on the inside? In other words, it opens toward you. To use an analogy here, just go have a look at your front door when you're inside the house. In most instances the front door opens in. Our souls resemble our houses in the sense that we are on the inside, and we decide if or when to open the door. Once again, let's use our imaginations here and compare our bodies, which consist of our heart and soul, as the core to our inner sanctum. Let's refer to our bodies as our houses or temples. This temple is the place where we live and usually feel safe. Inside this temple is a door, which we can choose to open or close to the forces outside. We can let in whomever we want just like we do when we allow people to come into our homes.

Now I want to ask you another question. When do we know that someone is calling or wants to come in? They knock, right? Well, this also applies to the door to our soul.

There is a knock that we can hear or refuse to hear. It is ever so faint. It is also very persistent. It's a beggar at the door. Do you know the beggar who is knocking? That beggar is your very best friend trying to get in to help you clean up your house. That beggar is eager to work side by side with you. He would like you to do some dusting along the way in order to make the transition into your next life as easy as possible. That beggar loves you. He knows all that you are capable of and all that you can be because he knows you inside and out, even better than you know yourself. That beggar knows that "it's the constant and determined effort that breaks down all resistance, sweeps away all obstacles."[15] That beggar understands how frightening it is to let him in because after you do, you can no longer claim ignorance as to what is going on in your life. Once you open the door and let him in, you will be able to see what needs to be corrected or cleaned up in your life. It is a big step to open the door, but don't be afraid to make it! "The greatest mistake a man can make is to be afraid of making one."[16] If you're afraid, you can take your time. You may open the door only a small crack if you choose, but once you open it, it will remain open. You would not want it any other way. In fact, you will eventually open the door as far as it can possibly be opened because the warmth and brightness of the light you let in will only bring

32

you warmth, peace, comfort, and all the good feelings that come as a result of being able to better see in the light. "The person who goes farthest is generally the one who is willing to do and dare. The sure-thing boat never gets far from shore."[17]

I think deep down inside we all know who that beggar is—it is our Creator; it is God. It is up to each and every one of us to open the door, if only a crack at the beginning, to let him in. *Tap, tap!* God loves each and every one of us with an endless love and with such a profoundness that is beyond our human comprehension. *Tap, tap!* He will never stop knocking because he cares so much for us as his children. He wants to make sure that we do things right and according to his will. He knows what is best for us. He knows that the greatest form of love is discipline. At times he answers our prayers with a "no," but he always hears them and always answers them one way or another. God also knows that he knows best because he can see with a divine vision that we cannot. When we open the door, we learn discernment and have the benefit of that vision or wisdom, but first and foremost, it is necessary to open the door and let him in. You will learn that "the intensity of your desire governs the power with which the force is directed."[18] *Tap, tap!* Yes, it really is there. Try to slow your life down. Just sit a while and listen

33

for it. Okay, I know that you hear it now, even if it is ever so faint. I know that your house might be in quite a mess, but this visitor doesn't mind. He's seen messes before and does not shy away from hard work. Open the door just a crack and you will see just a glimpse of the bright, shining, and oh-so-eager face asking to come in. "It sometimes seems that intense desire creates not only its own opportunities, but its own talents."[19] Yes, I know that there is some work to be done, but isn't it wonderful that there is someone so willing to help you with it? One of my sisters often uses the quote, "Many hands make for light work." This definitely holds true here as well. You are not alone. Just open the door and you will soon see! "Choose the way of life. Choose the way of love. Choose the way of caring...Choose the way of goodness. It's up to you. It's your choice."[20]

Step 2 ~ The door to our soul opens from the inside. We can use our greatest of all freedoms, our *gift* of free will, to choose whether we will open it or not. It's up to us, it really is! Here are a few more thought-provoking questions to help you out. The more questions we ask ourselves, the clearer the answers will eventually become. What are you doing to encourage a more positive life every day? Do you have a daily journal or quote book? Are you enjoying quiet time on a daily basis? Commit to keeping a thought journal and daily quiet time for a month and see how you feel!

My *No* Means *No*!

Our oldest granddaughter is now fourteen years old. I can't tell you the pleasure that she brought us when she was born. I had no idea about the depth of love grandparents could feel for their grandchildren until I actually experienced it. We have had seven more grandchildren since that momentous day, and we still hope to exceed that number. Not unlike the love we have for our children, the love for our grandchildren is equally as great. Every grandchild has such a special place in our hearts whether the first, the middle, or the lastborn. It has been said that love multiplies; it doesn't divide. I can vouch for that statement because it certainly has in the love we have known for our children and our grandchildren. I also know that love multiplies in all instances where it is present, not only with our families, but in other relationships as well. True love does not cause resentment, bitterness, or family friction. True love grows and embraces others in such a way that no one feels short-changed or robbed of their fair share of it.

When our oldest granddaughter was two years old, she was experiencing the terrible twos. It is the stage of life when a young child hears a lot of the word *no*. I have a grandson who is now two years old, and he is also hearing the word *no* often. I also notice that he is using it more than his fair share. At times, it can be seen as a battle of the wills, as he refuses to do what is asked of him. I smile to myself because he is so strong-willed and defiant, but on the outside I remind him that my *no* means *no.* His parents are reminding him on a daily basis, so I must follow suit when he spends time with us to make sure that we are on the same page as far as what is acceptable or unacceptable behavior. We all know that these two-year-olds understand the meaning of the word *no.* We also know that a lot of the times they just want to defy the authority behind the word. When our first grandchild was two years old, our daughter utilized the expression, "My 'no' means 'no'" quite often.

One time in particular the reverse happened. My husband and I were visiting them, and we were laughing and tickling our then two-year-old granddaughter. The more she seemed to enjoy it, the more we wanted to just squeeze her and tickle her some more. I guess it got into the point where she had had enough because she said *no* to us so that we would stop. We thought that we were still playing the "tickle me" game, so we proceeded to tickle her one more time. She turned around and looked at us and said in no uncertain terms, "My 'no' means 'no.'" Even at the young age of two we knew she meant it. We respected her wishes, and we stopped tickling her. If she not only understood those words at such a young age but could effectively use them and get the results she wanted, why does the proper use of this word elude some adults? It has been my experience that few people realize the appropriateness and, at times, very valuable need to actually use the word *no*. Saying *yes* to everything all of the time is no more appropriate than saying *no* all of the time, regardless of your age. It's perfectly okay to say *no*, at least some of the time, if you have a good reason for doing so. If you are uncomfortable with a person/situation or what is being done to you or asked of you, just say *no*! If you are not taken seriously the first time, just like our young granddaughter, look the person straight in the eye and say, "My 'no' means 'no.'" We heard her loud and clear.

Did you know that discipline has been said to be one of the greatest forms of love? When someone is saying *no* to us, it may actually be for our own good or for theirs. It seems to me that we have confused the meaning of a lot of words in the English language. I don't know how many times the word *no* is used incorrectly. At times it is used to actually mean the word *maybe*. Similarly, others may use the word *yes* but they actually mean *no* or vice versa. It is necessary to have a good look at these three simple words of *yes*, *no*, and *maybe*, and make every effort to use them appropriately. When we really mean what we say, there will be little or no room for confusion. The misuse of these three simple little words can end up getting most of us into a lot of hot water. "Mean what you say" and "Say what you mean" are handy mottos to use in everyday living. By walking to the beat of this drum, we benefit by having more open and honest relationships. This results in better communication with others. There is a big up side to this type of communication because it is better for all the people involved to know what the boundaries are in a mutually respectful relationship.

We eventually end up with a lot of positive things like self-respect, mutual respect, personal responsibility, and also accountability when it comes to our own actions. "Success on any major scale requires you to accept responsibility...in the final analysis, the one quality that all successful people have...is the ability to take on responsibility."[21] I have a beautiful message that I would like to share with you. It was written by Whitney Griswold and adds to what I have to say in an incredible way. "Self respect cannot be hunted. It is never for sale. It cannot be purchased. It cannot be fabricated out of public relations. It comes when we are alone, in quiet moments, in quiet places, when we suddenly realize that, knowing the good, we have done it; knowing the beautiful, we have served it; knowing the truth we have spoken it."[22]

Don't you just love the words in this message? I sure do. When we have self-respect, it gives us the desire, the confidence, and the ability to effectively use the word *no*. It is our God-given right to be able to say *no* even if there are negative consequences.

When you develop self-respect, the inner positive effects for standing up for yourself or what you believe in more than make up for any negative fallout which may result from saying *no*. I know that it sounds simple to use this little two-letter word, but it is actually quite difficult. First of all, we have to practice our use of it. When we use the word *no*, it must always mean *no*. There can be no exceptions. If at a later date, we change our minds from a *no* to a *yes*, we must take the time to explain why we have changed our response. If we don't, we lose some of our credibility. For example, we should use the word *maybe* if we are unsure, and we should utilize the words *yes or no* if we are sure. When we properly use these three simple little words in the English language, those around us know where they stand. If the people around us also used these three little words the same way, we would all know where we stand with each other. John D. Rockefeller, Jr. said, "I will pay more for the ability to deal with people that any other ability under the sun."[23] His words are a pretty strong indication of how difficult getting along

41

with people actually can be. There would be a lot less frustration in our lives if we all followed this simple advice. "Hold yourself responsible for a higher standard than anybody else expects of you. Never excuse yourself."[24] It is up to each and every one of us to make every effort to develop responsible behavior when dealing with those around us. Our words are so important, but two of the smallest yet most important ones are *yes* and *no*. When we give our word it is necessary to keep it in order to have both self-respect and the respect of others.

Step 3 ~ Make sure that you "mean what you say" and "say what you mean". If your "*no* means *no*" stand by it! People will eventually take you at your word and your self-esteem and self-respect will increase, thereby allowing you to command more respect from others. Once again, here are a few more questions that you can ask yourself to better benefit from my simple suggestion of recognizing the difference between "mean what you say" and "say what you mean". Often times, the difference is ever so subtle, therefore, it is necessary to be really tuned in to your inner self. When we are more honest with ourselves, we end up with more honest relationships with others. Do you remember a time when you said *no* but meant *yes*. Or when you committed to an engagement that you knew you weren't going to make? How did that make you feel? Try planning your days so that you can be sure to allow enough time for your family, friends, and yourself! This will help enhance your ability to be true to your word and true to yourself.

Hiss...My Name is Gossip

I already know that this is not going to be an easy chapter to write; however, I also know that it begs to be written. Do any of you have a pet peeve of one kind or another? Well, I have to admit that I do. I know that I have more than one, but one of my biggest pet peeves is the act of gossiping and the damage it does. This is one of those subjects, that no matter how hard I am going to try, it will be very hard to flower up.

The first thing I need to do is remind everyone of the power of communication. I know that in my last book I wrote about it quite extensively, but I only want to touch base on it by telling you a couple of short stories in this book. Many years ago, I took a class on effective communication. During that class, the professor wanted to demonstrate to the students just how much our words can change as they are repeated from one person to the other. He proceeded to get about ten people to go up to the front of the class. He then whispered a sentence into the ear of the first student in the line. After this, he instructed the student to whisper the sentence to the next student in line. Each person was to continue this process until the sentence got to the last person down the line. Subsequently, the professor asked the first person to repeat the sentence he or she had heard at the beginning of this procedure. Then the last student was asked to do the same thing. I cannot tell you how different the sentence was when comparing what the first student said to what the last one did. Words got changed all the way down the line.

The second little story I am going to tell you is a true story as well. One day my husband was golfing with his lifelong friend. Over the years we had also become friends with his wife, and we got together many times as couples. On one particular day, this man told my husband that his wife's elderly father had suffered a heart attack. When my husband got home from his golf game he proceeded to tell me that our friend's father-in-law had passed away. Due to the fact that we had known this couple almost our entire lives, we knew each other's family quite well. Therefore, I then passed this information along to some members of my own family. It was then decided that we should send some flowers to express our condolences and show our respect. My husband and I happened to be visiting with this couple a day or two afterwards, so we opted to just deliver the flowers ourselves. You cannot imagine the expression on our friend's face when we arrived at the door with our gift and offered our sympathy on her father's death. Her father did have a heart attack, but he had not passed away. Somehow or other, my husband assumed that he had when he was told about it. When I received the information, I acted on it. Thank goodness these people were such good friends and no feelings were hurt. As red faced as we may have been, they were pretty amused by our blunder. A month or so later, her father actually did pass away, and they reminded us of the fact that we had already respectfully acknowledged his passing. This second story demonstrates that even as good as our intentions may be, we can still goof up and incorrectly repeat some information we have heard.

Now, I am going to get into the less desirable part of this chapter. News, whether it is good, sad, or bad can go into what I refer to as another zone. There is nothing wrong with repeating information that needs to be repeated. Usually it is totally appropriate to share information because this is how we communicate with each other. It's what we share, how we share it, and why we share it that makes all the difference between whether it is appropriate or not. This is the part I find most difficult to write because it is about a subject I find so negative and ugly. It's the subject of gossip. Gossip is very different from sharing news. Sometimes I think we all know the difference, and then when I observe some of the damage that gossip can do, I'm not so sure. Most gossipers pride themselves on being well intentioned when they repeat something they actually know they shouldn't. Others don't care. Gossip has the tendency to be more than the mere sharing of any kind of news because it involves a lot more extrapolation about the news itself by the person or persons passing it along. The gossipy one has the desire to give a lot of his/her personal opinions rather than just the facts.

It is very easy to fall into this trap. Subsequently, the person receiving this information may pass it along the same way or further add his/her opinions to it. Remember those ten students at the front of the class? Well, the misinterpretation or misrepresentation of what may or may not be going on in another person's life is what starts the rumors. It's what gets the gossip mill going in the first place. We all have the tendency, at one time or another, to be the receiver of gossip or the repeater of it. No one, no matter how good his/her intentions may very well be, has been exempt from gossip of one form or another at some point in life. There is no use pussyfooting around this topic. Gossip is a fact of life! A good rule of thumb to use before we repeat what we have heard is to ask ourselves if it is really necessary to do so. If the answer is *"no,"* then we must ask ourselves why we would repeat what we have heard and would we want it said about ourselves.

I have had the habit of cutting out many articles of interest over the years. This one is from a local newspaper. The message was of great interest to me then and still is to this day. I can't even say which local newspaper featured it, because one of our two main papers stopped publishing some time during the period I started to collect these articles, which was well over twenty-five years ago. The article itself is called "Nobody's Friend." In it, gossip is named as nobody's friend. It states that gossip has, "no respect for justice."[25] It goes on to say that it can "maim without killing, break hearts and ruin lives."[26] It indicates that the more gossip is repeated, the more it is apt to be believed. The unknown writer of the article says that the victims of the effects of gossip are powerless. It is almost as if, the more a victim tries to stop a rumor, the more impetus the rumor has. According to this article, gossip can "tarnish a reputation, wreck marriages, ruin careers, and cause sleepless nights, heartache and indigestion."[27] I cannot come up with any better words to describe what the author of this article had to say as far as the damage that gossip can do or the pain that it can cause. It can "make innocent people cry in their pillows."[28]

As far as I'm concerned, gossip can never be good. The unknown author of this article further proves this point by saying that gossip hisses just like its name. It includes all types of gossip; whether it is office gossip, shop gossip, party gossip, or telephone gossip. The article specifically states that "before you repeat a story, ask yourself, is it true? Is it harmless? Is it necessary? If it isn't, don't repeat it."[29] As far as I'm concerned, this is darn good advice. As difficult as I know it is to follow, making the effort to do so is all anyone can ask. People think that swords can hurt people and cause bodily damage. Yes they can, but words can be like swords that cut even deeper, so deep that some may never heal. I can't stress this enough! I found another little quote, which coincides with the previous mentioned article. In it, Tryon Edwards states, "To murder a character is as truly a crime as to murder the body."[30] He obviously feels as strongly as I do about the subject because in another quote he goes on to say, "The tongue of the slanderer is brother to the dagger of the assassin."[31]

I think I've made my opinion on this subject pretty clear. It's one of those topics that I felt really needed to be addressed. Due to the fact that gossip is so averse to me, I want to make this chapter as short and precise as possible. Remember, the key to stopping gossip is to know the difference between sharing news and sharing gossip. Once you figure this out and make a concerted effort to stop gossip, a lot less damage will be done. It has been my experience that if you refuse to gossip, eventually people will stop sharing gossip with you. This habit makes for cleaner living. You may not know everything that is going on, but ask yourself, do you really need to?

Step 4 ~ Gossip is never good no matter how you look at it! I'm suggesting a few more questions to further ask yourself. By doing so, you may get a better understanding of the negative consequences of gossiping and how you can avoid it. Have you ever repeated information you know you shouldn't? How did it make you feel? Make sure to surround yourself with people who genuinely care and love you and your friends. This is a great way to keep away from gossiping!

Mister Sun and Mister Wind

As mentioned in my Introduction, I classify myself as a motivational author. I have been inspired by the words and works of many other authors. With this inspiration in mind, I have now crossed over from "being motivated" to trying "to motivate" others. This theme of helping others is the basis and the end goal of all that I write. Have you ever heard of Coles Notes? When I was a student in high school and university, I found that there were condensed notes, covering a large variety of topics available in many book stores. When and if I couldn't find the time to do justice to a large text book or all the class reading requirements, I would purchase a booklet of Coles Notes on the subject that I was studying. These notes zeroed in on the most pertinent information a student would need to know on any given topic. While attending university, I was blessed with three young children and very little time to spare. These condensed notes were a Godsend to me in balancing my young family and my desire for a higher education. With all the information that a student needs to process, any help in this regard is a big bonus.

Condensed notes, on most topics, are great because they highlight the main points that a student really needs to absorb.

They narrow it down to what is really important; therefore, it takes less time for the student to scope it out on his/her own. When a teacher does this for a student, he/she cuts their work to a large extent. In my last book, I mentioned that it would be virtually impossible for a person to experience every facet of life and most wouldn't really want to. The wise person benefits from the experience of others. As a teacher, my books are being offered as a form of condensed notes to those students who are willing to benefit in this way. Albert Pine suggests "what we do for ourselves dies with us; what we do for others and the world remains and is immortal."[32] I agree with Pine in his assessment of giving our most important words immortality. I think, when writing motivational, non-fiction books, the desire for our words to live on with our loved ones is our legacy to them and to future generations. Therefore, their importance carries even more weight. These types of books are more universal in their scope because they can apply to a large number of people who may be seeking out different kinds of advice or counsel. Thus, in my opinion, I feel that my tips can be beneficial to others as well, and are not only applicable to my own family. This conclusion has been a huge motivator in inspiring me to share my self-help recipe in the first place. The steps that I have suggested to better cope with life or to find a happier self are the most pertinent information or points of interest based on my personal experience. I want to share all that I know with you in order to help make your life easier.

Every concept that I have shared thus far, at least in our culture, is what I would consider to be universal. We may not experience them all, but according to the feedback I have received, there is a point or two in both of my books that we can all relate to. I suspect that there is actually more than just one or two. The goal for me, as a teacher, is to narrow the information down into a practical learning tool. By doing so, you will have the opportunity to utilize the skills faster and easier. This will only add to life's enjoyment and enhance all that it has to offer. Remember, life is a gift. It is a gift that we should not take for granted. It is one that we should be very grateful for, and the first way to show this gratitude is by saying thanks. "Gratitude takes three forms: a feeling in the heart, an expression in words, and giving in return."[33] By embracing these three forms of gratitude, I now acknowledge and willingly accept the third stage, that of giving in return.

As I reflect and go through my own life experiences, I draw from the wealth of information that I have been exposed to over the years. I am using it to compose these condensed notes for you. This is my gift to all my readers.

Pick and choose what applies to you in your own life. These are only tools or guidelines that I have chosen to share with you because my aim has always been to help others in any way that I can or have been chosen to do. At this time, I want to relate a familiar story. It may not be quite as familiar to you as it is to me. I asked my daughters if they knew the story about Mister Sun and Mister Wind, and although they said the title sounded familiar, they couldn't recall the actual story. It makes me think that I never taught this story to my children or my students, but in actuality, it was taught to me at a very young age. It would explain why my daughters couldn't fully remember it. I am recalling it from a time long ago, but it obviously stuck in my mind for a reason.

In this story, Mister Wind had the tendency to be a big blowhard. He liked to brag about how great and strong he saw himself to be. Mister Sun was the exact opposite. He was the strong silent type who seldom said much about himself. He enjoyed listening to all those around him. One day, Mister Wind decided to boast a little more than usual and tried to get Mister Sun to agree to a contest or competition of strength with him. Mister Sun, being the nice, smiley kind of guy that he was, wanted no part of this game. Mister Wind refused to back down and kept trying to prove his point. He finally succeeded into goading Mister Sun, who just kept smiling all along, to make a wager with him about his perceived strength. He refused to agree that Mister Wind was stronger than him and allowed Mister Wind to try and prove it. Mister Wind looked around and happened to see a man walking alone down the road. He said to Mister Sun that he would prove his superior strength by betting that he could blow hard enough to blow the coat right off the man's back.

Mister Sun never said a word as Mister Wind blew and blew as hard as he could. It seemed that the harder he blew, the harder the man hung on to his coat. After Mister Wind was all blown out, he finally admitted that he was not able to blow off the man's coat. He wasn't overly concerned because he had certainly shown how powerful and strong he was, and he was convinced that Mister Sun would fare no better. Mister Sun knew, however, that "there's a period of life when we swallow a knowledge of ourselves, and it becomes either good or sour inside."[34] He was quite amused by all of the boasting. Then Mister Sun looked at the same man with the coat tightly wrapped around him and smiled. The more he smiled, the more he shone. The more he shone, the hotter the weather became until the man walking down the road could no longer stand the heat. He finally removed his own coat and put it over his arm. Mister Sun never spent one moment bragging about his abilities to Mister Wind. He just looked over at him and smiled. He didn't need to talk or brag because his actions proved his point. Mister Sun knew that there was no need to worry about whether or not the sun would rise and shine or the capabilities he had. He also knew that everyone should be prepared to enjoy the gentleness and warmth of his reach.

I love this little story. I know I do because it has been in my memory bank for over fifty years, and I have thought of it often. It's one of those stories, like the "The Tortoise and the Hare" that just sticks with you as the years go by. Sometimes in life it is necessary to remind ourselves of as many of these little stories as possible because the lessons learned in them remain as important today as they did in the past. "Effort only fully releases its reward after a person refuses to quit."[35] Make every effort to recall these stories as often as possible, and abide by the lessons learned. Your efforts will not go unrewarded.

Once again, I'm trying to appeal to the child in you. It has been said, "The best classroom in the world is at the feet of an elderly person."[36] I wish we didn't grow so old that we lose sight of these meaningful stories and stop referring to the morals gleaned from them in our daily lives. The moral to all these stories is eternal. I know that the "The Tortoise and the Hare" also deals with unappealing boasting, but the reason

I'm recalling the previous story is because I want to discuss the other moral that I see in it. Although I know that bragging and boasting is unattractive, it is apparent to me that both Mister Wind and Mister Sun represent something else as well. In my opinion, Mister Wind represents someone who doesn't know how to treat people. He seems to think he can get things done in his own harsh way. On the other hand, Mister Sun bathes this man in the warmth and gentleness of his smiling, shining face.

How many times are we similar to Mister Wind and have a harsh attitude toward others? The harsher we are the more guarded people are around us. Is this not what present day bullying is all about? When a person is gentle and kind with a sunny disposition, people can relax around him/her, and this makes for a more positive relationship. "What the dew is to the flower, gentle words are to the soul."[37] We've all heard sayings like, "You get more with wine than you do with vinegar," but over and over again we need to remind ourselves of this fact. How are you treating people? How are you coming across? I've heard people talk to others in the same tone or worse than the one they would use on their own dog. "I've learned that one should keep his words both soft and tender because tomorrow you may have to eat them."[38]

Take the time to really listen to what is going on around you and observe firsthand what I am saying. What kind of tone do you use with your children? Remember the little boy in the first chapter who needed time to "shake it off" just like his dad had taught him to do. Well, guess what? We are all teachers! There probably isn't a day that goes by that we don't have the opportunity to either learn something new or teach something new to someone else. So I ask you, what have you learned or taught today? Is it all that you wanted it to be? It isn't even so much about how you want to be perceived, but more about what kind of an example you are setting for those around you. Good teachers lead by example. Good examples have the same domino effect as bad examples. It is up to each and every one of us to treat people with love and respect. Eventually, those around us will follow suit. It is necessary to decide which role we will play. Mister Sun, Mister Wind, good guy, bad guy; it really doesn't make much difference what story or what names you use, because over and over again the message is the same. "Be beautiful inside, in your hearts, with the lasting charm of a gentle and quiet spirit that is so precious."[39]

At times, it is hard for me to fully grasp the importance of our role in life. We all have so much to offer those around us. We are all in a position to influence others by all that we say and do. Don't fool yourself into thinking that no one cares or that no one is watching. Children are like sponges as they absorb all the information around them. They don't miss much. We have a very powerful role in setting the proper example for the people in our lives. This role should not be taken lightly. Therefore, these steps that I am providing are my condensed notes to help you become a better student/teacher and to help you realize the importance of this role. "I want to help you grow to be as beautiful as God meant you to be when he first thought of you."[40]

Step 5 ~ Make a choice today on how you want to live your life. Mister Sun or Mister Wind....what's it going to be? It really is up to you! To discover all that you can be, it may be necessary to ask yourself a few more questions. What kind of image do you want to project? What kind of example do you want to set for those around you? Do people look up to you and want to follow in your footsteps? There is no greater compliment if they do.

Tap...Tap

I know that I have shared a lot of childhood stories with you to make my point. I have also shared a lot of factual stories for the same reason. I do this because I feel that it is easier to learn something if you have a picture in your mind to go with the point that I am trying to make. Pictures really do clarify the meaning of words. If we always use words to describe what we are trying to say or how we feel, their true meaning can get lost in communication or translation. By using imagery to get a message across, there is less room for misinterpretation. Peter Nivio Zarlenga says it best when describing the power of the imagination. He states, "I am imagination. I can see what the eyes cannot see. I can hear what the ears cannot hear. I can feel what the heart cannot feel."[41]

I want to use this kind imagery to help pull together the title of this chapter. I am going to describe how I view life somewhat similar to a totem pole. Early on in life, it would seem that most of us start off at the bottom of the totem pole. As children, we really don't give this concept a lot of thought. We all start off as babes and aren't responsible for ourselves for a number of years. As time goes by, with the combination of maturity, education, and experience, we move up on the totem pole of life. The more mature we become, usually corresponds with our growth in responsibility and accountability. Some people are slow learners, or some just prefer to take their time as they scale this imaginary totem pole. Some people actually have no desire to scale it at all while others don't realize that they have a choice. Yet some people are both aware and eager to take on the task. According to this image, there are plenty of steps all the way to the top of this pole. For those of us who choose to scale upward, we soon realize that "there is a kind of elevation which does not depend on fortune; it is a certain air which distinguishes us, and seems to destine us for great things; it is a price which we imperceptibly set upon ourselves."[42]

At the beginning, when people first realize that they want to scale it, they tap away at the bottom in an effort to move on up. Sometimes they have the notion that the higher up the totem pole, the more power they will have over their own life and the lives of those around them. Each step up the totem pole may be seen as a "life will be easier or a more powerful" step. In my opinion, they have the mistaken notion that life will get easier higher up on the pole. As previously stated, when at the bottom of the totem pole, in most instances, life is actually not too complex. However, as you move up the notches, frequently you can become not only more responsible for your own life but also for the lives of others in the process. Despite this fact, somehow or other, this process is still attractive to a lot of individuals.

For those who enjoy "60 Minutes", most of us recognize that Andy Rooney is seldom short of an opinion. I just love his wry sense of humor and I hope you do as well. He has an opinion on this topic too. It goes as such; "Everyone wants to live on top of the mountain, but all the happiness and growth occurs while you're climbing."[43] This is probably one of the best explanations for the desire to scale the totem pole of life in the first place. It is seen as a part of our personal aspirations and desire to succeed or feel fulfilled. However, as we continue with our endeavor, we soon realize that there is already someone above us on the totem pole. The person at the top realizes the magnitude of this job while the ones tapping to get there may not. When the climbers finally reach the destination they have been working toward and feel the exhilaration of scaling the totem pole, they are suddenly distracted as they try to decipher the sound that they are now hearing that disturbs their peace of mind. *Tap, tap*! There it goes again. *Tap, tap*! Life at the top of the totem pole is usually a lot more stressful than life at the bottom. As stated earlier, some people have the incorrect notion that life at the top involves a big job, big money, and less work. This is not usually how life works. According to Josh Billings, "Fame is climbing a greasy pole for ten dollars and ruining trousers worth fifteen."[44] Those who take on big responsibilities usually can't even make enough money for the load they have chosen to carry. Every step up the totem pole is a necessary step to reach the satisfaction that one may be searching for, but it doesn't mean to say that this is an easy endeavor. Alexander Graham Bell reminds us that it is wise to remember "The most successful men in the end are those whose success is the result of steady accretion...It is the man who carefully advances step by step, with his mind becoming wider and wider,-and better able to grasp any theme or situation, persevering in what he knows to be practical, and concentrating his thought upon it, who is bound to succeed in the greatest degree."[45] It is wise to remind ourselves that we have the freedom to make many personal choices. They can have a great impact on us and those around us but ultimately we are both responsible and accountable for these choices.

Can you see the picture clearer now? The more responsibility a person takes on, the more stressful a person's life can become. At times, the more complex a person's life becomes the more frustrated and short-tempered the person may be. These feelings can result in negative emotions, fatigue, and the whole spectrum of variables that can affect how we come across in our dealing with others. These factors contribute to our personal frame of reference and how we communicate.

Oftentimes when we use only words to communicate, the tone we are using can blur what we are actually trying to say or they may alter the meaning all together. We can say a good thing in a gruff way and totally alter the meaning of the words. Not only can our tone alter the meaning, but our facial expressions and body language can add to this effect. I also notice that having the benefit of e-mail correspondence is not a benefit at all in some instances. A message may not always be received in the spirit that it was intended. People have a tendency to interpret messages according to how they may be feeling at the time. This may vary several times throughout the day depending on what is happening in an individual's life. Effective communication is a very slippery slope to say the least. Whether a person is talking or writing, a message can be taken several different ways depending on the variables that I have mentioned, and these are only a few. I don't know if you are familiar with duplicate bridge, but in this particular format, the players are not allowed to bid out loud. They must use a bidding box. The reason for this is to even out the playing field between all players so as to eliminate voice intonation in the bidding process.

If some serious bridge players see a need to eliminate this variable, you can well imagine how often we use it during the day in the numerous conversations that we may have. I remember when I worked as a telephone operator and there was a need to make a public recording. My supervisor thought I had a nice voice and recommended that it be used to make this recording. The fellow who was preparing me for the part got me to record it over and over again until he finally had to give up. As nice as my voice may have sounded, this recording was supposed to be neutral, and I could not take the lilt out of my voice. I ended each sentence that I read on an up note like I had a smile in my voice, and I simply could not change that intonation. Although this was a positive sound in most instances, it was not the quality that was being looked for in this one. Therefore, even a positive tone can be inappropriate at certain times.

Whether on the giving end or the receiving end of any message, when we have a lot of stress going on in our lives, it is very easy for our vision to be clouded, our thoughts to be muddled, and our message to be unclear. This may have a huge impact on our verbal tone or the body language we use when dealing with other people or how we receive information that is sent to us either verbally or in writing. Communicating without considering all these variables is hardly communicating at all. *Tap, tap!* Can you hear me now? Some people think that communicating is as easy as ABC. All we need to do is look at the increase in the number of words in the English language and add a few of the previously mentioned variables to figure out; it is no easy feat. We have complicated life, and it's up to us to simplify it if the going gets too rough or tough. Keep it simple, that's my motto.

We all experience stress in our lives at one time or another. Simply put, it's a fact of life. One of the tools that I have found handy in order to better cope with it, is to do things in layers. I have coached my family to do the same thing. I find it similar to the concept of dressing in layers to combat cold weather. Many years ago when I was quite overwhelmed with all that I had going on in my life, I couldn't see the "forest for the trees." I found that the more stressed we are, the less likely we will be able to see what needs to be done to correct the situation. I agree with this statement by Booker T. Washington. "I have learned that success is to be measured not so much by the position that one has reached in life as by the obstacles which one has overcome while trying to succeed."[46] I have had plenty of obstacles on my path. I have failed on more than one occasion. It was the earnest desire to overcome and the achievement of overcoming these obstacles which gave me the true meaning of success. Without facing my fears and my failures, the rewards and exhilaration of overcoming them would not have felt nearly as successful.

Once I had the opportunity to clear my head, which was not an easy task, I discovered better ways of doing things. Instead of everything being so connected, I simplified my life by untangling all the different things I needed to do. "For the resolute and the determined there is time and opportunity."[47] I started to look at things more logically instead of so emotionally. This is a very necessary step. It's what I would consider to be the first step in removing unhealthy stress from life. Everyone needs to prioritize what's going on in their lives. With all the double income or single parent families, everyone seems to be overwhelmed with life in one way or another. It is very difficult to work full time, raise a family, and manage a home all at the same time. So many people are burning the candle at both ends in this regard. I was doing the exact same thing and it took me a while to figure out the problem and even longer to come up with some possible solutions. When we are overtired it is hard to be unemotional and sometimes we can become irrational about a lot of not so important things. We need to mentally organize ourselves about what really needs to be done. Over and over again, I find the common theme of people being overtaxed by what is going on in their lives. They find themselves struggling to keep up. Are you one of them? Do you really need to do everything that you are doing? Do you really need to have everything that you have? Do your children really need to be involved in all the extra-curricular activities, etc.? There seems to be an endless number of questions that you actually need to ask yourself. There is a huge difference between really needing to do something and feeling you need to do something because everyone else is doing it! This is where true self-analysis and evaluation come in. "Your only obligation in any lifetime is to be true to yourself."[48] If some activities are less necessary than others, remove that layer. Free up some time. It is a good idea to not feel so rushed and harried most of the time. "The indispensable first step to getting the things you want out of life is this: decide what you want."[49] This is exactly where I started in my healing process. In order to better cope with my life and remove some of the unhealthy stress, I had to recognize and acknowledge the situation first and then go from there. A problem can only be solved once we admit we have a problem. It took me a long time to admit that I couldn't keep up with all the demands in my life.

Cutting down on some activities is one thing, but an equally important factor to consider is our money situation. I realize that the cost of living has gone up; however, if our money is spent on a lot of toys instead of the basic necessities of life, is it possible to take a layer of stress off in this department? A person can be working so hard to buy items that they have no time to actually "play" with them. My goodness, there are only so many hours in a day. Why work long hours, which may take from quality family time, to buy something that we may seldom have the time to enjoy? It really isn't that difficult to figure out. Try to remember that "money will buy a bed...but not sleep, books...but not brains, food...but not an appetite, finery...but not beauty, a house...but not a home, medicine...but not health, luxuries...but not culture, amusements...but not happiness, a crucifix...but not a Saviour, and a church pew...but not heaven!"[50] By simplifying our lives on a lot of fronts, we can decrease the stress all around. Take time to think before you act.

At every opportunity, before you go ahead with a new job, a job promotion, a bigger house, or some other purchase, take the time to ask yourself if this choice will make your life easier or not. "Virtue consists, not in abstaining from vice, but in not desiring."[51] It is so easy to get on the treadmill of life or in the rat race that we can actually forget that we are supposed to be enjoying life. It is necessary to take a very hard look at our lives and decide what we can live without. You might be very pleasantly surprised. Eliminate one or more of these things, and you will relieve some of the negative stress factor. You could be a pioneer by starting this trend amongst your own peer group. Bigger, better, and more of are not always the wisest choices. More quality couple time, more quality family time, and more quality alone time may very well eliminate the need for a lot of what I consider to be unnecessary baggage. Assess and reassess. Take off a layer here and there, and before you know it a lot of unwanted stress will be removed. You won't feel so *tapped out*. Don't expect it to be easy either. It takes a long time to get ourselves in the fixes we're in, and things won't or can't change overnight. Undoing what we've created takes a lot of work as well and "history has demonstrated that the most notable winners usually encountered heartbreaking obstacles before they triumphed. They won because they refused to become discouraged by their defeats."[52] Try your best to untangle your life, and in the end you will feel a personal victory, which in itself is a success. It's just a different kind of success. By painting this picture, I hope it gives a more accurate idea of how we can contribute to our own stress. My goal is to give a few tips to help alleviate some of it. Perhaps, when we have a better look at our situation, we can get a better idea of what is causing our problems so that we can actually remedy the situation.

Step 6 ~ Stress is a real killer. There is good stress and bad stress. Decide which is which and the *tap, tap,* will feel a whole lot better. On a more positive note, if you're having trouble managing the amount of stress you feel, try something different. Pick up a new hobby like painting, yoga, running, or cooking! These hobbies are all wonderful stress releasers.

The Happy "Snipper"

For those of you who haven't figured out that I'm an early riser, I want to let you know that I am usually up at the crack of dawn. This is a blessing in disguise for my husband who is snoring away in the bedroom. Now he will not be attacked by all my verbiage when he gets up. He is no morning person. Sometimes I feel like I am lying in wait to have him listen to all I have to say when he finally does get up. This is the time when I listen to my oh-so-soft music. It is also my best thinking time, although my husband may beg to differ. When the ideas start flowing, I find it hard to resist the urge to write them down. One of my friends gave me a book to read titled *The Red Hot Typewriter* after I shared my first book with him. If I was in the same league as that author, my book may very well be considered *The Red Hot Keyboard*.

Although there is no smoke coming out of my computer just yet, if I keep this up there may very well be. That's the optimist in me. However, I must admit that my typing skills are improving somewhat over time as I peck away at the keyboard in front of me. "You learn that, whatever you are doing in life, obstacles don't matter very much. Pain or other circumstances can be there, but if you want to do a job bad enough, you'll find a way to get it done."[53] If there is one obstacle that I am trying to overcome, it is to better my typing skills. I know from past experience that, "all things are difficult before they are easy"[54]. I am forever grateful to my husband, because once again, he has strength where my weakness lies. There is no way I could get this job done without the help of his computer skills.

Before I get into the "meat and potatoes" of this chapter, I want to tell you that I've decided to write the whole book before I let anyone read it. In my first book, I tried the strategy of allowing my husband and my daughters to read the chapters as they were written for the first half of the book. My husband teases me when he says to keep pumping out these chapters, but I think he's figured out that my writing flows much better when I do just that. It's not to say that he has no input in what I am writing, it's only to say that he will have to be patient and wait to read what I haven't written just like everyone else. There is a definite strategy to this approach. I want to see firsthand if this book really grabs him. Hopefully, he will be unable to put it down, and then I will know if it is a good read or not! He doesn't know it yet but the second part of this strategy is to see if what I have written is of interest to the male population. He's actually my "guinea pig" so to speak. Guys need some help finding good coping skills too. I want this to be a generic book, not just for the feminine audience out there but more for the general population. As different as we may think we are, there is still a child in each of us that reaches out for help from time to time. According to Josh Billings, "Life consists not in holding good cards, but of playing those you hold well."[55] I believe that everyone needs a little coaching now and then, to help play the hand that they have been dealt, male and female alike.

Have any of you ever seen the movie *Being There* about Chauncey Gardner starring Peter Sellers? If my memory serves me correctly, this is not one of his typical comedies like *The Pink Panther* series or *A Shot in the Dark*. The one thing that sticks out in my memory the most about the movie, although it has been years since I've actually seen it, is that Chauncey, the main character, was a gardener. He absolutely loved gardening, and he just loved talking about it. I think Chauncey knew the true meaning of gratitude. He seemed to be living the philosophy of being "more aware of what you have than what you do not. Recognizing the treasure in the simple - a child's hug, fertile soil, a golden sunset. Relishing in the comfort of the common - a warm bed, a hot meal, a clean shirt."[56] However, somehow or other, people got confused about what he was trying to say. They thought he was this brilliant man expounding on all sorts of philosophical views, and all he was doing was talking about his garden and the joy it brought him. In this movie he was just a simple man, enjoying a simple task, yet people were seeing him as some kind of genius.

I truly appreciate Chauncey's message. I have always had a penchant for gardens, but I must admit that contrary to the movie, gardening is no simple task. One of my earliest gardening experiences goes back to the age of about six. It was a wet spring. As the snow melted, the pleasure of wearing rubber boots and wading through all the puddles was, as my five-year-old granddaughter would say, "this is the best day of my life" kind of experience. My childhood friend of the same age was with me at the time when we decided that walking in wet mud was an even more enjoyable experience than wading through water. In those days, almost everybody had a backyard garden because families were generally larger and money was scarcer. I came from one of these typical families. Our backyard garden was just perfect to enjoy some of my kind of fun. I proceeded to go right into the mud and quickly started to sink. Before I knew it, the mud was fast reaching the tops of my rubber boots. Either my friend or one of my siblings decided that I needed help. At that time, there were five children in my family, or four with a baby along the way. When my mother came rushing out of the house with these big rubber boots on (probably my dad's) and a shovel in her hand I knew that I was in trouble. She was fit to be tied! Needless to say, my friend got sent home, and I got sent into the house. In spite of this negative experience, deep down inside, I knew there was a gardener in me. I have been honing this skill ever since.

The previous experience actually only further piqued my interest in gardening techniques, as I started to help out with the picking and cleaning of a variety of vegetables over the years for my mom. Although, have you ever noticed that whatever someone else has always seems to look or taste better than what you have? When I was twelve, another one of my friends and I decided that perhaps we should raid the neighbor's garden to just prove this point. I struck out again! In the dark, I managed to cut my ankle on a broken piece of glass. So great was my fear of telling my dad what I had been up to that I went to bed with a bleeding ankle and never said a word. Needless to say, I had to fess up the next morning. I had to go get stitches after all and I soon realized that getting caught doing something wrong was a mighty fearsome thing. Even in those earlier years, I was already practicing the art of not being perfect and have done so many times since in spite of my efforts to do otherwise. I do agree with Thomas Carlyle when he says, "Of all the acts of man, repentance is the most divine. The greatest of all faults is to be conscious of none."[57] I'll tell you one thing for sure. It has never made me feel good inside to engage in inappropriate behavior, and after these two occasions, I was mighty sorry. I knew that I had done something wrong. As a child, I didn't actually know at the time which was worse, doing the unacceptable act or getting caught at it. These couple of childhood pranks were no big deal, but even at that young age, I knew full well the difference between right and wrong. The main thing I soon figured out was that, even if I never got caught, it didn't make what I had done right or make me feel any better about it.

Sometimes, even as adults, we still try to lull ourselves into believing if we don't get caught in an undesirable act that it's all right to engage in it. Don Herold states, "Moralizing and morals are two entirely different things and are always found in entirely different people."[58] It's not uncommon to find people who are quite willing to preach but who are either unable or unwilling to practice what they are actually preaching. This is why I have chosen to use the word *teach* in my introduction versus the word *preach*. For some reason or another, I find it easier to digest. It is not easy to live an exemplary life. The less said about it though and the more done to live up to what you believe in carries more weight. "It is a great deal better to live a holy life than to talk about it. Lighthouses do not ring bells and fire cannons to call attention to their shining - they just shine."[59] Actions really do speak louder than words! I love what Louisa May Alcott says when speaking about herself, "Far away there in the sunshine are my highest aspirations. I may not reach them, but I can look up and see their beauty, believe in them, and try and follow where they lead."[60] To follow where these aspirations lead, one must act and go where the dream takes you.

After my husband and I were married and we eventually bought our first home, I decided to take up a more legitimate form of gardening. I have become somewhat of a decent gardener, but it has been no easy task. I've also managed to pique my husband's interest in gardening, much to his initial aversion to it. Not unlike me, he had the opportunity to help out in his parent's garden. One task that he disliked a great deal was the harvesting of potatoes. I remember a few years back when we went to a family reunion and he got up to say a small speech. Lo and behold, if he didn't tell the story of how much he dislikes gardening. He said that almost every time he turns around I have him out there planting, fertilizing, watering, pruning, weeding, and whatever else I can think of for him to do. According to Janice Elice Hopkins, "gift, like genius I often think, only means an infinite capacity for taking pains."[61] If there is anyone that has taken the pains to enhance our garden it is my husband. The ironic thing about it is that he now sees things that actually need to be done without my asking. He has put in more garden edging, hauled more rock, and done more work than I could have ever thought possible. He has even volunteered his services for other less capable people in our community. At times, I even have to ask him to stop.

Boy, sometimes we really do have to watch what we wish for because we just might get it. Don't tell anyone, but he has even made a gate in our fence that backs out into a field behind our backyard that is owned by the city. We have started to plant out there too. I am starting to think I am married to Johnny Appleseed himself. I know that he says he built this gate for me, but when I can't see him in the backyard, I know just where to find him. This garden of ours has become our therapy for whatever ails us. There is always something to be done, and if it's not in our yard, watch out neighbors, here we come! "Personal relationships are the fertile soil from which all advancement, all success, all achievement in real life grows."[62] Needless to say, my husband and I are cultivating the soil for more than one reason. We've discovered that when a couple decides to work together, their relationship can blossom as well.

Still to this day, if I find that I am frustrated with something negative going on in my life, all I need to do is go out and dead head flowers. Before you know it, I'm in a better mood. When my granddaughter was younger, she tried to dead head flowers too but not for the same reasons as me. She proceeded to snip off live flowers with those little fingers of hers faster than I could get the word *no* out of my mouth. I notice that my husband now does the exact same thing, as far as using gardening to vent. He used to vacuum with a vengeance when he was frustrated with work, but now he gardens to take the place of work. Francis Bacon says it best, "He that will not apply new remedies must accept new evils: for time is the great innovator."[63] I know that he would never admit it to anyone, not even to me, that he likes it at least a little bit. I've come to the conclusion that no one would do the amount of gardening he does if he didn't. He must be enjoying all this garden work because he is helping me create a live painting of the way I want my garden to be. Both of us have a set of pruning shears, and I can't tell you the pleasure it brings me as we snip away in our garden each spring to start off the new growing season.

It has been said that "the real secret of happiness is not what you give or what you receive; it's what you share."[64] My husband and I not only share but take personal pride in our gardening experience. I notice that my son-in-law has stopped calling me "old black thumb" the way he did earlier, so obviously somebody with more skill has kicked in. My husband has even gone so far as to buy himself a new pair of rubber boots. You know the kind. They're the black ones with the orange trim. I just hope that he doesn't go out when it's really muddy. I may have to rely on my trusty shovel to dig him out just like my mom dug me out all those years ago. I'm just glad that I bought myself a pair of those handy dandy rubber boots too. Kids...don't we ever grow up?

I must admit though, that we are not only happy "snippers," we are also happy rockers. We have a wonderful swing in our backyard. Actually we have two, one on the deck and one farther out in our backyard. We use both depending on which way the sun is shining. We feel quite honored to be able to call ourselves "swingers." We take regular breaks to swing and talk. According to Allan Loy McGinnis, "There can be no intimacy without conversation. To know and love a friend over the years you must have regular talks."[65] I couldn't agree more! After we talk, we work some more. It's not only my girlfriends and I who have

84

solved some of the world's problems. My husband and I do our fair share right in our own backyard. We also walk daily, just like I do with my southern girlfriends. We all have some negativity in our lives. What better way to get rid of it than by turning it into a work of art? Once you get the hang of it, it grows on you. After a while, you just do it for the fun of it, like we do with our gardening and our walking. "Wisdom is knowing what to do next, skill is knowing how to do it, and virtue is doing it."[66] Before you know it, the experience of producing something positive takes over and replaces a lot of so called negativity in our lives. The fact that we have found a project we can work at together has added to our joy. We don't all have to become happy "snippers," but there are plenty of creative ways to channel negative thoughts and feelings. You just have to find the right ones to suit your own needs and creative abilities. Martha Washington has an interesting philosophy. She says, "I have learned from experience that the greater part of our happiness or misery depends on our dispositions and not upon our circumstances."[67] William James reinforces this by saying, "Human beings can alter their lives by altering their attitudes."[68] Every one of us has negative life cycles, but with a little effort and patience, we can turn them around.

Step 7 ~ There are so many wonderful ways to better communicate in any relationship. Some are more artistic like gardening, while others like rocking on a swing might be considered more relaxing. There are also numerous creative ways to better communicate with those around us. Chances are you will create a masterpiece of one kind or another if you tap into your creative abilities. Once again, take the time to ask yourself a few simple questions. What do you enjoy doing? What kind of time frame do you have to devote to your desire to build closer, more intimate relationships? What do you have in common with the person/people that you enjoy and what can you build on in order to enhance each other's lives?

God's Wife

The other day I received an e-mail from an old friend whom I hadn't heard from in years. It wasn't a personal one. It was just one of those e-mails which, for whatever reason, you decide to share with someone. I was very grateful to receive it as it made me think of him fondly. It also jarred me into writing this chapter. I hope this doesn't scare people off from writing or saying things to me. I know that I have a memory like an elephant and you never know what may end up in one of my books.

Not everyone has a computer or access to e-mail, so perhaps this little story will be as new to you as it was to me. This is a synopsis of the e-mail my friend sent me. I have no idea if it is a true story or not. It's about a woman who spotted a barefooted little boy about ten years old looking through a shoe store window sometime in December in New York City. She asked him what he was doing as she got closer. He told her that he was asking God for a pair of shoes. The woman proceeded to take him by the hand into the store. She picked out several pairs of socks and then asked the clerk for some water and a cloth so she could wash the boy's feet. After doing so, she bought him a new pair of shoes. She helped him put on a pair of socks and the shoes. She then gave him the remaining pairs of socks. The little boy was so grateful. When he looked up at her with tears streaming down his face, he asked her if she was God's wife. Isn't that a neat story?

It reminds me of another little story I heard many years ago in my teaching days. It was about a priest that made a special visit to a classroom during a catechism lesson. It was always an extraordinary thing to have such a special visitor. After speaking to the class, the priest asked if there were any questions. There were the usual questions that any child might ask and the priest easily answered them. One little boy, however, eagerly had his hand up and could hardly wait for his question to be answered. Finally the priest called upon him. The little boy asked if God was married. The priest was momentarily speechless, but then he asked the boy "why" he would ask such a question. The little boy answered from his own experience and in such a logical and sincere way. He said, "Well, he must be married because who would tell him what to do if he wasn't?" Of course, he would need a wife to do that! Out of the mouths of babes come some of the most innocent of observations and comments. I find it very amusing that due to the male image of God, some children from their own perspective may see him as a husband and probably as a family man. Actually, I not only find it amusing, I find it somewhat endearing and refreshing as well. It actually brings me joy, for "joy is the echo of God's life within us."[69]

I have always gotten such a kick out of children and their unpredictability. If there is one thing I know about children it's that we should make every effort to get to know them and how they might behave a little better before we set ourselves up in any kind of public way. I particularly know this from my experience with my own daughters and grandchildren. I also have some fond memories from my teaching days. One such memory is about a little boy from the second grade class that I was teaching. We used to have the occasional school concert or talent show and asked the parents to attend. An older sister in the school had decided to call upon this little boy to be in the concert. She wasn't a teacher, but she volunteered to do some of these kinds of tasks in order to help out. I was quite surprised that she had chosen this particular boy. From my previous observations, if there was any trouble to get into, he was usually in the middle of it. She rehearsed several hours with all the children so they would perform well in front of all the parents who came to see the concert. When it was this young boy's turn to go up to the front of the school auditorium and perform, he pulled a fast one. When he saw such a fine audience, he decided to tell an off color joke instead of what he had rehearsed. Everyone in the audience broke out into some kind of laughter or varying degrees of discomfort. I can assure you, there was no one more uncomfortable than that older sister. She was totally dismayed that this boy would do such a thing, yet I wasn't one bit surprised. As previously stated, I had more experience with children, and I also knew this little boy well.

I remember another time even farther back, when I was actually about the same age as this little boy. We were in church and the priest was asking several questions to the young congregation in preparation for the sacrament we were soon to receive. It has since been my experience that the more eager the hand is flailing to answer a question, the chances are the answer to the question may be a little more "out there" than most. That day, the priest decided to ask the children where they thought their soul was and up came the eager hand of another little boy I knew well. He was not only a fellow classmate of mine, but he lived a couple of doors down the street from where I lived. Bright as a button and quick as a flash, he answered "at the bottom of my shoe." Even at six years old, most of us knew that although his answer was mighty funny, it was not quite the one the priest was expecting.

Both this priest and that older sister got sucked in by these two little ones. I thought it was so neat. I must have a weird sense of humor because I got such a kick out both of them. I have a sneaking suspicion that I wasn't the only one. Do you think that God might find these children any less amusing than we did? Not the God I know! It is wise to remember as you experience some of the growing pains that we all do when it comes to our own children, no matter how old they get, they are still just that, our children. So here are my questions to coincide with the previous stories. As we age, do we become so old that we are no longer considered to be children of God? Would God lose his sense of humor in dealing with us and some of the silly questions that we might ask at any age? Perhaps, I should have asked this question first. Don't you think that God himself has a sense of humor? I once read that he must have, because after all, he created us didn't he? The God I know, love, and serve is a mirthful God. He smiles, laughs, and enjoys us as his children, yet he suffers our pain too. This image of God has brought me untold pleasure. So I ask this yet again, as our children age, do they become our children any less? To me, the answer is "*no*." Therefore no matter how old I get, I continue to see myself as a "child of God" and in that very same light. Must we allow ourselves to be stunted by the fear that it is inappropriate to ask questions or to offer an opinion if one is asked of us at any age? I've come to know that "nothing in life is to be feared. It is only to be understood."[70] Will God be any less amused or less loving because of it? Not in my books. "Trust in God. Believe in yourself. Dare to dream."[71]

I know though, that "nothing happens by itself...it all will come your way, once you understand that you have to make it come your way, by your own exertions."[72] As children, we are allowed to ask and answer many questions with such innocent freedom. As educators, "what we want is to see the child in pursuit of knowledge, not knowledge in pursuit of the child."[73] I have always loved being referred to as a "child of God." I am grateful for the wonderful knowledge of how much he loves children. From my own childlike vantage point, I too have questioned many things. I know that as a "child of God" it is okay with my Father. Norman Dowty confirms this by saying, "You are infinitely dear to the Father, unspeakably precious to Him. You are never, not for one second, alone."[74] Oftentimes, his love has been referred to as similar to a mother's love for her children. This pleases me every bit as much because I am not only a mother but a grandmother as well. What greater compliment could God give women than to compare his love to ours?

I saved an article from our local paper, which has become yellow with age. It was written by Tom Harpur who often wrote on different religious views. In it he states that over time we eventually take on the personality of the God that we worship. For some people, it appears to be in our human nature to strive for greater things. In doing so we make every effort to unite with the human perception of the God we know, love, and serve. If we see God as harsh and judgmental we adopt those same characteristics in our dealings with people. We can become self-righteous and oftentimes see ourselves above others. If we see God as forgiving and merciful we strive to have more of these kinds of attributes. We have a greater desire to embrace others with empathy and compassion. Therefore, I suggest that you take a moment and ask yourself how you view God. Are you eager for judgment day because you regard yourself as being on the right side of the line? Are you almost as eager to see some people get their just desserts? I realize now that I feel so much more comfortable and at peace in knowing God as loving, kind, and merciful. I take great comfort in knowing that he loves me with an infinite love whether I'm perfect or not, which is beyond my human comprehension. At times, he may very well find some of the things I say and do somewhat amusing, but hopefully seldom disappointing, as I make every effort to be pleasing to him. Please try to remember that we are created in the image and likeness of God. We reflect this image to the world in all that we say and do.

I find that men and women can view things in such different ways. They not only have different views, they have different ways of saying things. It reminds me of a book, which is based on the theory that women are from Venus and men are from Mars. Many times when my husband and I discuss as we walk or as we swing, I see some of those differences. We were made in different ways for a reason. My husband says I have a tendency to flower things up when I have something to say. I consider this to be the eternal gardener in me who wants to spare everybody's feelings. He has a tendency to cut to the quick and has been referred to as brutally honest when he was in the business world. When I search through my quips and quotes to emphasize what I am writing about, I can't help but snicker to myself as I think of some of the unprintable ones that my husband has saved over the years. It's a good thing that I'm writing this book. Between the two of us, I soften his edges and he hardens mine so that we can effectively deal with all that life has to offer. I need his strength, and he needs my softness. Our marriage, in most instances, consists of a healthy balance between the two.

Once again, I can honestly say that I have been no different than the children mentioned earlier in this chapter. This may sound silly, but I have actually felt sorry for the Pope. As I have looked at the church and its all-male hierarchy, I see the absence of the softness of the female influence. There is no way that I would want to make so many powerful decisions for so many people without my husband's male influence, nor would he without my female influence. We are constantly bouncing off our ideas against each other. We do this with other people whom we trust as well. I love the stories I've told in this chapter because it helps broaden the view of our image of a loving God. Perhaps only the children feel safe and secure to ask or answer these kinds of questions. I have a question that I often ask myself. Don't we all have to become like children in order to enter into the kingdom of God? I was taught that it was a matter of a loss of faith to question anything, but I have come to know that "a belief which leaves no place for doubt is not a belief; it is a superstition."[75]

Searching for truth in our desire to have a better, more profound relationship with our Creator is an act of faith, not a loss of it. It has been said, "Faith is the ability to see the invisible and believe in the incredible, and that is what enables believers to receive what the masses think is impossible."[76] Faith is the process of overcoming fear and embracing the true wonder of the love of God. It takes a lot of courage to think outside the box. Nevertheless, please remember that everything I write in my books is food for thought and should be seen as such. I don't have all the answers, but I feel much safer asking questions than I would have at an earlier age. This, to me, is an example of my "faith" in a loving and merciful God.

I truly feel that there should be more of the Venus (female) influence at the Vatican, because in order to have a balanced structure of any kind, you need both. There, now I've said it. It took a while, but I finally got it out. I know I've overstepped myself here because no one asked me a question, but I've eagerly had my flailing hand up for quite a while now. Well, sometimes you just have to blurt things out, so I am. It is a question that begs to be both asked and answered, even if the powers that be aren't willing to listen. It just feels good to get it off my chest! Personally, I don't think God would be offended by any child who thought he had a wife. For all we know, he might even take it as a compliment. I agree with Doris Leasing when she says, "Think wrongly, if you please, but in all cases think for yourself."[77] I may be totally wrong in the way that I think, but I have the God-given right and ability to think. For that, I am forever grateful. Freedom of thought and freedom of speech are gifts. Daniel H. Burnham states, "Make no little plans; they have no magic to stir men's blood and probably themselves will not be realized. Make big plans; aim high in hope and work, remembering that a noble, logical diagram once recorded will not die."[78] Even when I wrote my first book, I planned on writing this one as well. I also planned on sharing these food for thought ideas. "Once freedom lights its beacon in a man's heart, the gods are powerless against him."[79] In spite of my gentler nature, I do have a tendency to see things logically as well. Some things in life make more sense to me than others. In my opinion, one of these things is the need for a more powerful female influence based on respect and equality in all walks of life, including the church.

I have a little confession to make. In spite of all the fear that was instilled in me in my younger years by the priests or sisters who helped shape my personality, there is strength and determination which comes from within that could not be quashed. It's what I refer to as the rebel in me. When I first met my husband at sixteen years old, it was already exhibiting itself. Once a month on Friday, the entire school population would attend Mass. In those days, the boys and the girls were always segregated with all the boys sitting on one side of the church and all the girls on the other. I took my rightful place by my future husband's side (even at sixteen I knew he was the one for me) on the all boys' side of the church without a moment's hesitation. It's hard to believe that this incident took place well over forty years ago and how much closer I now am to sixty instead of sixteen. No one said a word to me or forced me to sit with the other girls. Most of us had boyfriends in the same school, but to my recollection no one else sat beside her boyfriend.

I don't know why I got away with such a rebellious act; although, I didn't view it as one at the time. I just sat by his side where I felt I belonged, and I never felt one bit self-conscious about it. I now realize that I was ahead of my time. The rebel in me has been there for quite some time. I have learned to embrace it because it is an intricate part of my personality. It has been said, "Do not follow where the path may lead. Go instead where there is no path and leave a trail."[80] I am who I am for a reason, perfect or not. I also know I have a purpose in life that is unique to me just like each and every one of us does. It is finding that purpose and acting accordingly. Always, try to remember the power we have in shaping the personalities of others in our lives, including our own. This power must be acknowledged first, in order to be in a position to use it wisely. Take care to do just that.

Step 8 ~ We need to strive to think more like children. We might all be very surprised by what we observe from our childlike innocence and perspective. It's a good thing and it can be very refreshing. It is our God-given right, and no one should be allowed to take it from us. Therefore, on that note, try to spend a moment or two with your inner child as often as possible. Try your best to remember what it was like to be this child and how easy it was to please you. Ask yourself this simple little question to help you find the way.

What is something that is small but you love very much? Do something simple that makes you happy!

Good News

By the time you read this chapter you may very well already know my good news, but I need to share it with those of you who don't. Obviously all of you can tell by what I have written thus far that this is my second book. When I wrote my first book, I really had no idea if anyone, other than those closest to me, would actually find it worth reading. Although not too many people had read it, I decided to get a more objective opinion by sending my manuscript to a couple of publishing companies. "You have to leave the city of your comfort and go into the wilderness of your intuition…What you discover will be wonderful. What you discover will be yourself."[81] To my great astonishment and pleasure, both offered to publish it. I never expected to find myself back at work at this stage of my life, even if it is in the comfort of my own home.

My husband and I are very comfortable with living in a condo and although it is quite spacious, I find that I need more of a proper environment in order to "pump out" these chapters, to quote my husband. Sometimes I feel like I'm a gentle form of a volcanic eruption. Ideas keep flowing like lava into my mind, and I not only have the desire to write them down but also a need to do so. After some discussion with my husband, we are giving great thought into turning our small spare bedroom into an office for me. The contents of my red notebook, once kept in my night table, are now spilling out onto the spare bed. We are trying to be creative in figuring out how to use this small space so I can have what I need without sacrificing the bed that we require for our visiting family. This really is beyond my wildest dreams, but I must admit because of its newness, it is also frightening. "If we let things terrify us, life will not be worth living."[82] I'm sure that there will be some challenges ahead. You must, however, "accept the challenges so that you may feel the exhilaration of victory."[83]

I want to share a little about my style of writing with you so that you can better understand the need for some office organization. Over the last twenty-five years, I have collected numerous quips, quotes, stories and newspaper articles. Up to this point, I have just taped them in my red notebook or stuffed them into envelopes and put them in my night table drawers. Needless to say, at times it is very difficult to find the exact quote I am looking for because I have so many to sort through. For obvious reasons, I have chosen to save the quotes that coincide with my own belief system. All I need to do is search through them to find the right one to go along with the stories that I have to tell. Sounds easy, doesn't it?

Well, not exactly, because I'm finding it is taking a lot less time to just write about my own "isms" than to search through my hodgepodge of quotes to back them up.

Not to worry though, because now with the bright idea of getting a little office space for myself, I'll be better able to organize the chaos of my stash and possibly "pump out" even more chapters. Now isn't that a frightening thought? That's a rhetorical question, so there's no need to answer it. I much prefer to bury my head in the sand when it comes to my book writing capabilities. As red-hot as my keyboard might get, so far my audience is few and far between. If I actually see this second book published, you just never know what a little encouragement could do. To put things in my own words, you just might be surprised about what I can "spit out" next!

Well, enough about that! There are those who may not share my sentiments. Right now, my husband is downstairs in his office working on his stamp collection. He has been an avid stamp collector since he was a young boy. Just as we finished lunch, he asked what I planned to do for the rest of the afternoon. I answered his question with a question just to be sure that we were on the same wavelength. I asked him what he planned on doing. When he said that he was going to work on his stamp collection, I quickly said that I guessed I would just work on my book. He responded by saying that it was exactly what he hoped for. So somehow we both managed to get our own way. This is what I consider to be the true spirit of compromise. I'm jesting now when I say that I notice he doesn't have a bed in his office. Yet, if things go as planned, we all know that I won't either in the not too distant future. I have been asked a few times throughout our marriage just how do I get this husband of mine to do all the things that he does for me. My answer is, "Blackmail, sheer blackmail!" Very early on in our marriage I told him in no uncertain terms, if he didn't behave himself I would lick his stamps while he was at work. The biggest nightmare of every true stamp collector is that a new stamp would become a used stamp. Mint stamps are far more valuable. It has worked wonders. Strategy…whatever works. My goodness! We all need to have a little playful fun in our marriages once in a while, especially when we're getting into the long term ones.

I've started off on a very light note in this chapter because if you are anything like me you enjoy good news. Some of us actually enjoy the good news of others as much as we enjoy our own good news. Just yesterday, when we took our five-year-old granddaughter to her ballet class, I noticed the pleasure on the faces of the other little girls as each one did a small informal performance. They not only showed pleasure when performing themselves, but also in what they saw their peers doing. Watching the children react this way actually brought so much pleasure to me as well. I couldn't help but smile to myself. Oh, once again, to see life through the eyes of a child. What happens to us as adults that changes the way we see things? This, I believe, is an age-old question. All we need to do is go back to the story of Cain and Abel from the Old Testament to know that sibling rivalry, jealousy, and envy amongst our peers are feelings that are as old as the day is long.

To truly share in the success and joy of others would be such a wonderful thing. Many of you may remember the story about Joseph with the cloak of many colors. It's about the jealousy Joseph's brothers had toward him and what ensued as a result of this jealousy. It also tells about Joseph's goodness and how he reacted to the mean spiritedness of his brothers. My husband has a cute little expression he used often when our children were younger as they compared themselves to each other. He told them that they "needed to keep their eyes on their own fries." We all seem to have the tendency to compare ourselves to others, especially our own siblings. We look around and see something that they have as more than what we have. We then think that life isn't fair. I can honestly say that I really don't know whether life is fair or not. One thing I can say is that I believe it to be just.

"Justice is the insurance we have on our lives and our property; obedience is the premium we pay for it."[84] Things happen for a reason, a reason beyond our human understanding, but probably for our own good. I do know that some things are beyond our control, but I also know that we have the power to change the things that are in our control. It takes wisdom to know the difference. If we look around and see someone that is more successful than us it is usually within our power to change our own circumstances. Rather than develop a "woe is me" attitude, we are far better off to create some good news of our own. "Destiny is not a matter of chance; it is a matter of choice."[85] Louis Pasteur agrees when he says, "Chance favours the prepared mind."[86]

I remember reading a cartoon in the comics one day. One frog was saying to another frog that he felt like asking God how he could let all the poverty and hardship go on in the world today. His friend, the other frog, said, "Well, why don't you just ask him?" The first frog replied that he was afraid to because God might ask him the exact same question. This answer puts the onus of the condition of the world right where it belongs. Remember that "the highest reward for a person's toil is not what they get for it, but what they become by it."[87] How many people actually expect God to fix things for them when they aren't really prepared to do anything to help fix things for themselves? "The people who get on in this world are the people who get up and look for the circumstances they want, and, if they can't find them, make them."[88] It is up to us to make a difference and work toward the greater good. According to an English Proverb; "the hand that gives, gathers."[89] There is no better reward than to see the results of our own labor. Another cute little joke that comes to mind is about a man who kept going to church, praying to God to let him win the lottery. Week after week, he would go to church, kneel before the altar and pray to win. Finally, on one of these occasions, a loud voice boomed out from the back of the church, "Buy a ticket!" Yes...it is up to us to act. We can't be winners if we don't do the deeds to become winners.

Sometimes, we can actually be silly in our expectations of God. Therefore, I really am glad that I see him as having a sense of humor as indicated in the previous chapter. I realize this little story is only a joke, but how many times do we pray for something good to happen to us but we don't really do anything to help make it happen? Miracles can happen, but they take time. They also may take some effort on our part. Bob Richards states, "Ingenuity, plus courage, plus work, equals miracles."[90] Remember, it is up to us to not only pray or think about something but to act. If we don't like something going on in our lives, a change might make all the difference. How many times have you heard the statement "the rich get richer"? I realize when most people use this statement they are talking about money; however, I'm not talking about money when I refer to it today. There are all kinds of riches in life that have absolutely nothing to do with money. Frequently people associate wealth with happiness. I'm not so sure that wealth is one of God's greatest gifts. Perhaps it is a good idea to take stock of what we have rather than what we don't have. This is not always easy to do.

One of my sisters once said that most of us do feel jealousy and envy throughout our lives at one time or another. She went on to say that it's what we do with these negative feelings that make the difference. If by chance you feel that someone, whether it is a sibling, friend, co-worker, or even an enemy has something in life that you might want, you have every right to seek out similar things. Just remember, wanting and trying to have what another person may have is all right as long as you don't take from them or destroy something in their life to get it. Jealousy and envy are human emotions. Acting on those emotions in a negative way is what causes all the problems. We were born human with the full spectrum of human weaknesses and frailties, but we were also given plenty of gifts and good qualities. We have choices in life because one of the greatest of these gifts that we have been given is free will. In my opinion, it's best to admit how we feel rather than deny it. Once we realize what we are working with, we can act accordingly.

I want to end this chapter with another story. I have always had a great respect for history and our heritage. In North America, there is a large native population. This is a story that an older Cherokee man told his grandson. I have no idea if it is a true story or not, but I know it is a good one. He told his grandson about the battle that goes on inside people. The story is actually called "Two Wolves." The grandfather explained to his grandson that inside each one of us there lives two wolves. One of them is evil. He explained that evil consists of all those negative emotions like envy, jealousy, anger, and so on. The grandfather then went on to say that the other wolf is good. This good consists of all the positive emotions like love, joy, peace, kindness, and so on.

The little grandson was quite impressed with this battle between the two wolves. He eagerly asked his grandfather which wolf won the battle. The old Cherokee man simply looked at his grandson and replied, "It's the one that you feed." Isn't that the truth? I do not think I can come up with a better way to explain good or bad emotions and how we deal with these emotions. How we react to the good news of others is a good measuring stick in regards to which wolf we are feeding. Are we truly happy for those who succeed? Do we share in their joy? Generally speaking the good that we do is rewarded one way or another. It doesn't necessarily mean to say that we engage in an act of kindness to get something back. It just means that acts of kindness may be bestowed upon our loved ones down the road. It has the domino effect. I believe that the more good we do, the more good that will follow. I can only say this, if we feed the good wolf, good things will happen in our lives. It really is up to the individual to decide which road he or she is going to take. The reward is the feeling of goodness that comes from within by engaging in the more appropriate behavior. I agree with Ralph Waldo Emerson when he says, "The reward of a thing well done is to have done it."[91] It is up to each and every one of us to decide which wolf we are going to feed. Once you decide, the rest comes easier! "I don't know what your destiny will be, but one thing I know, the only ones among you who will be really happy are those who will have sought and found how to serve."[92] There is no way that I could have said it better! Giving to others can be an extremely rewarding experience. Sharing in the joy, success, and good fortune of others is one way to give.

Step 9 ~ Make good things happen in your life and more good things will come. In so many cases, although not in all, it really is our own choice. It all depends on how we choose to look at things and what we do about it. Some simple suggestions I recommend are as follows; try your best to always stay positive! Try doing positive affirmations every day in the mirror, or leave yourself notes to remind yourself to stay positive.

Four Rooms

As I head toward the last four chapters, I find that once again I have more topics to cover than I first expected. I didn't have room for this subject in *I'm Not Perfect and It's Okay*, so now I have to choose carefully to ensure that I cover the most pertinent ones in this book. If only in my opinion, I am trying to prepare the best possible condensed notes in order to help all those who are willing to read them. The reason for doing this is because I have found that "in seeking happiness for others, you find it for yourself."[93] Once again, I must stress that these pointers may not apply to everyone; however, I believe the bulk of them are universal. I suggest that you pick and choose those that apply to you and adjust them to suit your own needs. I'm quite satisfied that most of us are exposed to at least one or more of the topics I have chosen to cover. Albeit, it is always a wise idea to customize any or all suggestions to better fit the individual. In fact, there probably is at least one lifestyle recommendation in either of my books for everyone. The key is to zero in on what suits you or to focus on what applies to you in your own life. Obviously, the skills I have attained are a result of learning to better cope and manage my own life. They are here for the asking. Not all people are asking;

therefore, we must always respect each other's choices. "As human beings, we are endowed with freedom of choice, and we cannot shuffle off our responsibilities upon the shoulders of God or nature. We must shoulder it ourselves. It is up to us."[94] In due course, if people are struggling with their lives, they eventually do reach out. My goal is to reach back at that time. "In helping others, we shall help ourselves, for whatever good we give out completes the circle and comes back to us."[95] Once a full circle has been completed, I know that I can comfortably move on and the healed person can now offer the same kind of guidance they received from me. In doing so, a chain of positive behaviors and events will link us all together in a creative and constructive way. True healing begins with ourselves.

In the last chapter, I wrote about the Cherokee grandfather who was explaining life to his young grandson. In Canada, we have come to call the people who were here first as First Nation people. They have asked to be referred to in this way. When we were young we always referred to them as the Indian people. Over the years, this has become a derogatory term to describe our oldest ancestors. I notice as we travel through the United States, especially through the southern states, that the First Nation people refer to themselves as Indians. We have visited many Indian Craft sales along the way and have enjoyed many facets of their culture. The signs are made by the Indian people themselves and displayed as Indian Arts and Crafts. I have a love for the Indian people as I do for all people no matter what they choose to call themselves. The reason I have gone into this preamble is because I want to share a little story with you about an Indian philosophy that I read about many years ago. I don't want to say that it is a Cherokee, Cree, Erie, Apache, or any other particular tribe/Indian philosophy because I don't know which one told the story. I also don't want to offend my Canadian First Nation people by calling it an Indian story, nor do I want to take from the American Indian who has not asked to be called otherwise. Its origin may very well be from the American Indian. "A man's feet should be planted in his own country, but his eyes should survey the world."[96] I would like to share this story with all those who can identify with it and appreciate that it was told by an older person in order to spread the wealth of his/her wisdom.

It has been a long time since I have read this story, and it is not one that I have kept in my night table drawer. If I don't explain it perfectly, it is not for lack of trying. The Indian or elder in this story was describing that each of our bodies has four rooms in it. The elder goes on to say that these four rooms are spiritual, mental/intellectual, emotional, and physical. The spiritual room, of course, consists of our faith and our relationship with our Creator or God. The mental room is comprised of our education, our knowledge, and our desire to learn. It deals with our intelligence. The emotional room consists of the happy times, the sad ones, what brings us the greatest pleasure, what makes us angry, and any or all emotions that we could possibly feel. Not all emotions are positive; nevertheless our human nature is comprised of the full spectrum. Last, but not least, is the physical room where we concern ourselves with our actual body and the condition that it is in. According to this wise older Indian, in order for each of us to have a healthy, well-balanced life, we must enter into each of these rooms on a daily basis. If we don't do this, our lives will not be as peaceful and as harmonious as they can be. Each area of our lives must be satisfied in order to find true happiness. "Remember when life's path is steep to keep your mind even."[97] It's not to say that we won't have hardships to face, it only means that if we are a more balanced person we will have better skills to cope with what may come our way. It has come to my attention that one of the most difficult things for us as human beings is to find that balance. As previously stated, with the stressful and busy lives that a lot of us lead, it may be hard to really find the time to follow the sage advice that is being offered. Although,

I must admit, that by not at least trying to follow some of it to a small extent, it will be hard to truly enjoy life to the fullest. "There is no achievement without goals."[98]

I would now like to go into each room, one room at a time, to explain what is there and how you can enhance your own lives by visiting what is actually within yourselves. The first room is the spiritual room. It is the room where we develop our relationship with a higher power. As stated in my first book, for those of you who believe in this Supreme Being, you may choose to call him/her by a different name. To make my point, I am going to call mine Bonhomme (a French term of endearment with special meaning to me). In this spiritual room, we spend time praying or talking with God. It is our faith room. We don't spend all our time in this room because if we did our lives would be out of whack. Although I feel that it is the first and most important room, I also realize that in order to have a well-balanced life I can't live/visit here all of the time.

According to the elder, I must also visit the other rooms in my body/house. Nonetheless, every day I love to spend time with the one who gave me life and who created me in his image and likeness. "While faith makes all things possible...love makes all things easy."[99] I start off my day by being thankful for both these gifts. Many times throughout

117

the day, I may re-enter this room. I especially like to visit here at night just before I fall asleep to once again give thanks or to pray for those in my life in need of prayer including myself. It is in this room that I become fully alive. In our local newspaper I have read many of Karen Toole-Mitchell's articles, which I discovered on the faith page. She has a Masters of Divinity degree. She was previously self-employed in Soul Seasons, a counseling and consulting partnership. In one of her articles subtitled "Fully Alive" Toole-Mitchell states that she has observed that some people live normal lives in extraordinary ways. In doing so, she feels that they live divinely inspired lives because they have explored their spiritual roots and have found the freedom to grow from this inspiration. Toole-Mitchell adds that because of this, these people take time to reflect on their lives and share what they have learned. To share who we are and what we believe in means taking risks. I couldn't agree more. To decide to step outside of our comfort zone and express ourselves more openly about our faith and spirituality creates a state of vulnerability. This is why I feel that it is a big decision to enter into this ordinary room and do extraordinary things! "For greatness after all, in spite of its name, appears to be not so much a certain size as a certain quality in human lives. It may be present in lives whose range is very small."[100]

I love this room because no matter how small and inadequate I may think I am, I feel God's presence and accept His Will for me. Although, I come to this room daily, I cannot nor do I want to stay in any one of the four rooms all of the time. I would not accomplish much else in my life if I chose to do so. In this room, I have found my faith and learned the art and value of balancing my life and enjoying what each room has to offer. "Nowhere can man find a quieter or more untroubled retreat than his own soul."[101]

The second room that I enjoy visiting on a daily basis is the room where I exercise my intellect. It is the room that I have used to better educate myself as well as challenge and develop my own intelligence. In this room, I can no longer claim ignorance is bliss. I have chosen to educate myself in such a way that I feel confident asking questions that at one time I wouldn't have dreamed possible. Finding the courage to do so has increased my faith, not only in a loving God but in myself. Stretching ourselves mentally can come in all forms. Although I enjoy reading and playing bridge, one of the forms I especially enjoy is in puzzle form. Over the years, I have taken great pleasure in developing my puzzle solving skills. The more I solve these puzzles the better I get at it. The better I get at it, the better I feel about myself and my own self-image. My favorite puzzles to solve are crosswords and crypto quotes. I also now enjoy Sudoku puzzles. Although they all bring me pleasure, the puzzle that has enhanced my life the most is the crypto quote. This quote is encoded by mixing up all the letters of the alphabet to reflect a different letter in the quote. By figuring out which letter stands for which, you can eventually decode the quote of the puzzle. I feel that I have been doubly blessed by having both the desire and the ability to do these puzzles.

First of all, it makes me feel somewhat intelligent to be able to do them as many people I've discussed this with say there's no way that they can. Secondly, and even more importantly, is the fact that most of the quotes I have saved and savored over the years are from these puzzles. Some of the wise sayings from several of the greatest thinkers that have ever lived or still live today have been found in these puzzles. I have had the double benefit of not only solving the puzzles, but I've personally gained from their sagacity. "Study without reflection is a waste of time; reflection without study is dangerous."[102] There are many ways to educate ourselves and some are a lot of fun, albeit challenging. Once again, I must stress that although I enter this room on a daily basis, I wouldn't want to stay in it all day. I may enjoy reading, puzzle solving, or educating myself, but I have other rooms to visit. I realize that "until input (thought) is linked to a goal (purpose) there is no intelligent accomplishment."[103] I must use what I learn in this room to better enhance my life and the lives of those around me. This has always been my main goal, and I am still making every effort to accomplish it.

The third room that I want to visit is the emotional room. I love and enjoy this room as well. It consists of the room where I laugh and where I cry, if necessary. Sometimes there is plenty to laugh about, and at other times there may be a sad event going on in my life that brings tears to my eyes. I deal with it here. This is an opportunity for me to also deal with all my other emotions. This is where I can admit that someone has made me angry or has upset me. I can also look at myself and admit that perhaps I have offended someone else, and I may need to say I'm sorry. In this room, I have discovered that there is a whole spectrum of emotions, which range from the very positive to the very negative. It is here that I acknowledge the full capacity of these emotions, and I take the time to decide which ones I will use to handle any situation that I may be facing.

Each of these rooms offers the opportunity to make different choices. In this room, I can take the advice of the Cherokee grandfather and decide which wolf I am going to feed. Remember that "you will become as small as your controlling desire; as great as your dominant aspiration."[104] I can choose between love/hate, laughter/tears, faith/fear, and every other possible emotional combination in all situations. It's okay to cry in this room if something sad is going on in my life. It is okay to know fear in this room and look for ways to overcome it. According to Eleanor Roosevelt, "You gain strength, courage, and confidence by every experience in which you really stop to look fear in the face…The danger lies in refusing to face the fear, in not daring to come to grips with it…You must make yourself succeed every time. You must do the thing you think you cannot do."[105] It's okay to admit anger in this room and figure out a positive way to deal with it. It is okay to admit that someone has offended me and how it made me feel, but I must learn how to love and not hate the person who made me feel this negative way. "We cannot despair of humanity since we ourselves are human beings."[106]

In this room, we not only have the right to face and deal with all our emotions, we also have the obligation. We must not only do it for ourselves but for the benefit of those around us. The less we deal with the things that negatively affect our lives the more power they have over us to negatively affect others. "The truth that many people never understand until it is too late is that the more you try to avoid suffering the more you suffer because smaller and more insignificant things begin to torture you in proportion to your fear of being hurt."[107] We are all far better off to take the bull by the horns and face what needs to be done rather than let our past have the opportunity to affect our present and future happiness. "The future is that period of time in which our affairs prosper, our friends are true, and our happiness is assured."[108] It really is okay to face up to a few things in this room. It's a well-known adage that the truth shall set you free. In this room, it is very necessary to be totally honest with yourself. It's okay if you don't always like what you see because then it gives you the opportunity and the real challenge to do something about it. It has been said that "The art of living lies less in eliminating our troubles than in growing with them."[109] Yes, it can be frightening but "it takes courage to know when you ought to be afraid."[110] No matter how scared we are to deal with something that is going on in our past or present life, facing it takes courage, and it should be seen as such. "Don't be afraid to fail. Don't waste energy trying to cover up failure. Learn from your failures and go on to the next challenge. It's OK to fail. If you're not failing, you're not growing."[111]

The last room that is necessary to visit on a regular basis is the physical room. This is the room that concentrates on the health and well-being of our bodies. I notice as the years have gone by that more and more people are concerned about this area. The concern is not only about exercise or the lack of it but also about the food we eat. We hear expressions like "You are what you eat." There is a major concern about the quantity of food that we eat as well as the quality of it. People can find themselves leading sedentary lives. Watching television, playing computer games, and other idle activities are adding to our sometimes poor eating habits. If we work long hours or have too much responsibility apart from work, we have little or no time to address this concern. If we are not in good health or do not have the time or the opportunity to enjoy some physical activity, we pay the price in other areas as well. That's the conundrum! It's finding or making the time to create a well-balanced person by addressing the needs of the whole person. "To be what we are, and to become what we are capable of becoming, is the only end of life."[112]

All four of these needs, whether spiritual, mental, emotional, or physical, are equally important and must be met in order to live a more centered and satisfactory life. If a person robs himself/herself in one area, it will have a negative impact in another one. By finding and achieving a healthy sense of balance in all the areas of our lives, a healthier sense of self will unfold. According to Thomas Carlyle, "He, who has health, has hope; and he who has hope, has everything."[113] It will then have the domino effect in our personal relationships, our family life, and our overall outlook on life. Energy begets energy whether it's positive or negative energy. People with positive attitudes attract people with this same kind of energy. "A kind heart is a fountain of gladness, making everything in its vicinity freshen into smiles."[114] The old saying "misery likes company" is the reverse of the above belief system. It actually can be true in a lot of instances. Those people who are unbalanced in their life style choices emanate a lot of negative energy. They end up attracting like-minded individuals. The end result consists of existing in a negative life cycle the majority of the time. A lot of people are reluctant to admit that they actually can do something about it to turn their lives around. This is another area where we need to be very truthful and honest with ourselves. We need to evaluate and reassess our whole lifestyle many times over. We must continue to do so on a regular basis in order to develop the balance in our lives that we all not only crave but need. It may take time and several attempts to achieve this healthy balance but "our greatest glory is not failing, but in rising every time we fall."[115] You may not succeed on your first attempt at entering all four rooms of your body on a daily basis, but keep trying. I promise that you will get better at it because "a will finds a way."[116]

Step 10 ~ Try your best to meet all the needs of your whole being, the spiritual, the mental, the emotional, and the physical. Once these needs are being met, a more positive, well-balanced life will follow. You will end up in the positive cycle of life. In the less positive cycles of life, you will have the skills to better deal with the situation. One of the first things to do is to set a few moments aside to ask yourself this question. Do you have a clear idea of what you want your lifestyle to look like? Sit down and write it out. Keep yourself accountable. Maybe even recruit a friend to do it with you!

The Skunks

For those of you who have not read my first book, I want to tell you that my husband and I are snowbirds. We go south for the winter, and we have just returned home after being away for several months. I must admit, it is not only the temperatures that are polar, but our lifestyles are as well. Now that we have returned to our northern abode and the temperature hasn't thoroughly warmed up, I have more time to sit at the computer and write down all the thoughts that have been coming into my mind over the last six months. I have so many fond memories, but if one sticks out in my mind it is this skunk story. Libbie Fudim's advice is sound when she says, "Recall it as often as you wish, a happy memory never wears out."[117]

Down south, my husband and I have so much couple socializing time as well as alone time for ourselves. In the past, we have almost felt guilty (me more than him) that we can get away from most of our responsibilities when we fly the coop and head south. We feel so fortunate in having the opportunity to do so. We find that the many friends and acquaintances we have made over time feel the exact same way. In the morning when my husband heads out to golf, which he does six times a week, I have spent my time developing lovely friendships with a few women who enjoy walking just like I do. We all seem to believe in the same philosophy of "don't walk in front of me, I may not follow. Don't walk behind me, I may not lead. Just walk beside me and be my friend."[118]

Every morning, we start off with picking up each other along the way, depending on where each of us lives. We walk over three miles pretty well every day except Sundays, which coincides with our husbands' golf games. Every year our friendships get closer and closer as we share more and more about ourselves. Yesterday, when we were visiting one of our daughters for the first time since our return north, she asked me which home we preferred. Talk about a loaded question! I told her it was impossible to compare apples and oranges. The lifestyle we have established by having two homes is what I call bittersweet. They are both exactly what we want and have worked toward, but they are at the opposite ends of the spectrum. We are sad to leave our southern friends, but the joy we feel with seeing our family and friends here, helps make up for it. According to C. S. Lewis, "Every day in a life fills the whole life with expectation and memory."[119] So here we are again at the end of one season and at the beginning of the other. We do realize, however, that "there is something in every season, in every day, to celebrate with thanksgiving."[120] Now we have the expected pleasure of being with our family and our friends in this season of our life, without giving up the memories of the life we have just left.

This chapter, however, is being written about our wonderful southern friends and how we have enhanced each other's lives. We have lots of couple friends, but this is about the women who have touched my life and the lives of those around them. "Love is everything. It is the key to life, and its influences are those that move the world."[121] Firstly, I would like to explain why I have called this chapter by its name. I'm sure all of you know just how much most women like to wear black. Usually, to offset the severity of this chosen color, the outfit worn will have some white in it. Personally, I seldom wear black, but seeing as those in our walking group usually do, I decided that I would too. One day, when we were all dressed in black and white, we met up with another woman that we didn't know who said that we looked like a bunch of skunks. We all laughed at the time, as we said aloud that we thought there were much nicer names to describe how we looked. Penguins came to mind! We have referred to ourselves, in jest, as "the skunks" many times over since that day. Although after that, we have had the tendency to jazz up our attire by not all wearing black and white at the same time because we didn't want to be called "the skunks" again. I can assure you that as we walk around in our retirement community, we are very hard to miss regardless of what we are wearing.

I must admit we are a habitual lot. I find that "goals are lines to the future. They allow us to run the race with the finish line firmly established."[122] To prove this adage, we, as a walking group, usually have the same goal in mind. We follow the same couple of paths every day depending on who is walking with us or if one of us has another commitment and needs to get home. One of the girls has even measured the distance, so we actually know how many miles we walk to ensure that we get in our workout as well as our fun. We enjoy walking by the golf course along the way and waving to our husbands. In my mind, it feels like we have become a bunch of high school sweethearts. We now have the opportunity to dwell on our own relationships with our husbands in this less complicated environment. Each of us seems so eager to spot our husbands on the golf course as we pass by.

The majority of our friends have been married for over forty years. My husband and I seem to be the kids on the block at forty years! When I look at all these long-time marriages, I find it hard to believe the statistics when it comes to divorce. It is so very enjoyable when we listen to each other as we philosophize on these morning walks. It has been said that "a friend listens to our words but hears our heart."[123] Every day is different. The topics we discuss have such a wide range. When we talk, we laugh at ourselves as we not only discuss, but solve, if only in our own minds, many of the world's problems. We have so much to say and so much to share, but who is really listening? I told these girls about my first book, and they were all so excited for me. I also told them that they would be in the one of the chapters of my next book, and here they are. Over and over again, we laugh, we share, and we talk about life. Mostly we know joy, but sometimes we know sorrow. At the end of each walk, no matter how serious some of our discussions may have been, we almost always end with the same joy we started off with. "The worship most acceptable to God comes from a thankful and cheerful heart."[124] None of us ever wants to forget this, and each day we are ever so grateful for the time we have spent together.

Each year as we meet up again, it's as if we have not skipped a beat. This is what true friendship is all about. We have come to know each other's children, if not in actuality, by what we know about them. We not only care about each other, we care about each other's families because "friendship is sharing openly, laughing often, trusting always, caring deeply."[125] We can relate to each other's experiences. We can identify with what is presently going on or that which has gone on in the past in all of our lives. These walks have become therapeutic for us all. "Happy is the friend who knows what to remember of the past, what to enjoy in the present, and what to plan for the future."[126] We have discussed so much of our past and shared the present with each other. Every year we also look ahead as we plan or talk about our future season together.

When I first met one of these girlfriends, it was toward the end of the first season. She and her husband were leaving in a few days, but she gave me her word that the following year she would get to know me better, and she certainly has kept it. She is now one of my fellow "skunks"! It is through her that I have met some of the other girls. This kind of kinship has had the domino effect. We have met more people since then who have become our friends as well. This is what our friendships have become because "our lives are filled with simple joys and blessings without end. And one of the greatest joys in life is to have a friend"[127] or several of them!

I remember my dad once saying to me that we can count the number of true friends we have in a lifetime on one hand. I feel very fortunate to say that I need more than one hand to count mine. Hopefully I may one day need a few toes too. I do agree with him because true friends are very hard to find. Orison Swett Marden describes it best. He says, "No young man starting in life could have better capital than plenty of friends. They will strengthen his credit, support him in every great effort, and make him what, unaided, he could never be. Friends of the right sort will help him more - to be happy and successful-than much money..."[128] I've also been told that we really discover who our true friends are when we experience some kind of hardship. I personally believe that true friendship is greater than this. I have a little plaque on my kitchen wall, which states, "Friendship shares the joy and divides the sorrow."[129] It is truly a combination of the two! When someone is genuinely happy for our success, we really have the opportunity to recognize the value of a true friend. This, to me, is the greatest test of the quality of a friendship. True friends are faithful, both through thick and thin, for "the better part of one's life consists of his friendships."[130] It is always wise to recognize the gift that these friends bring into our lives.

Although it is our southern friends that have inspired me to write this chapter, I must also acknowledge the wonderful friends whom we enjoy in our northern hemisphere. Friendship is something neither my husband nor I have ever taken lightly. I still have two of my first girlfriends who have been in my life since the age of six. Many years ago, these long time friendships blossomed into couple relationship. The solidity of these friendships has resulted in many animated discussions over the years as we toss around our ideas on a wide range of topics. No matter how vibrant some of these discussions may be at times, we have always managed to respect each other's right to view things differently from ourselves. We continue to this day to get together on a regular basis for some good food, good company, and the occasional verbal sparring.

Most of the time we agree, but sometimes we agree to disagree. This works too. I concur with Johnny Cash when he says that "happiness is being at peace, being with loved ones, being comfortable. But most of all, it's having those loved ones."[131] It is about being grateful for having family and friends in your life! Happiness, to me, is also about being able to be myself around those loved ones. It also means that it is wise to take care not to build my happiness on their unhappiness. I try my very best to always keep this in mind. "Whatever our creed, we feel that no good deed can by any possibility go unrewarded, no evil deed unpunished."[132] Life really does have a way of balancing itself out. One of my sisters always uses the familiar quote "what goes around comes around." In my opinion, we really can't give away a kindness. A fellow co-worker used to see it the other way around. One of her favorite sayings was "no kindness goes unpunished." I much prefer to look at the world from the positive point of view, how about you?

This preference of mine also includes people in my life who may not be my friends. I feel, that not only our friends must be treated like the fine gems that they are but we should make every effort to consider all other people's feelings in what we say and do. Thomas Merton says it best, "Happiness is not a matter of intensity but of balance, order, rhythm and harmony."[133] In my first book, I wrote about choosing our friends wisely. This is a continuation of that philosophy in the sense that it is very rewarding to be chosen as a friend as well. Life is not meant to be a popularity contest but rather an opportunity to be there for someone, in the same way that we would want them to be there for us.

Some personalities require less people in their lives. This is okay because their needs may be satisfied in other ways. Generally speaking, those who need more people or friends in their lives, find each other because like-minded individuals usually gravitate toward each other. No matter the choice, friendship usually gives the desire to strive to be all that people see us to be. At this time, it may be a good idea to ask yourself why your friends have chosen you to be their friend in the first place. It is also wise to expect from ourselves the types of behavior that we expect of others when it comes to friendship. It is wonderful to positively touch the lives of everyone we meet if only in some small way for all people pass through each other's lives for a reason. Remember that "a candle loses nothing of its light by lighting another candle."[134] It is always good to brighten a person's life even if they don't recognize exactly what we are doing and why.

There are many fine characteristics that I can use to describe what I like about certain friends, but the one that stands out the most is that of being kind. Kindness is all encompassing. When we truly love people we usually will go to great lengths to perform small acts of kindness throughout our lifetime. Helen Keller so aptly states, "Remember, no effort that we make to attain something beautiful is ever lost. Sometime, somewhere, somehow, we shall find that which we seek."[135] The something beautiful that we should all try to attain is to bring the qualities of true friendship into the lives of those around us. Just because someone is not our friend doesn't mean to say that we can't be theirs. This is the way to have true friends. You need to be one first! It may take a while for someone to recognize what you are offering, but trust me, in time someone will and the circle of true friendship will embrace you. "The future belongs to those who believe in the beauty of their dreams."[136]

Step 11 ~ Cherish your friendships. The only way to really do this is by being a true friend yourself. Be kind. The sound of laughter, the pleasure of sharing, the knowledge of being understood and accepted, are immeasurable. These are all forms of kindness. Friendships are so important. Commit to doing something special for your friends occasionally. Try setting aside time to make a special dinner or send a hand-written card.

YY

I am about to do something very strange. I am actually writing two chapters at the same time. My husband and I just finished spending the day with our grandchildren, and although I'm not quite as fresh as I usually am in the morning, I feel the need to write what I have to say. My oldest grandson, who is now ten years old, has a biblical name. He suits it too. It is the name Isaiah. Isaiah is the oldest of four children. Not unlike many difficult names that are hard for young children to pronounce, Isaiah has been given the nickname ZZ, pronounced the American way like Zee-Zee. When ZZ was about four or five years old, my husband and I had the opportunity to take him to a baseball game. My young nephew, who was about twelve at the time, was playing in a baseball league and ZZ really looked up to him.

I don't know if you are aware of the behavior of most four or five year olds, but several times as the game progressed, ZZ would ask us why this guy did this or why this guy did that. There was a woman sitting in front of us who finally turned around and rolled her eyes at us. I guess she couldn't believe how many times he asked why this or why that. Perhaps she couldn't believe the patience we had in answering all of our grandson's questions. Finally, even grandpa's patience wore thin because he turned and said to our grandson, "Your name should be YY instead of ZZ."

Sometime around the age of fifty, my husband and I had a neat conversation on one of our morning walks. I recall it quite vividly as he said to me that for the first fifty years of his life he was so easy going and accepted a lot of things at face value. Although he is a man with a strong character, he is also a very quiet man as mentioned many times before in some of the other stories I've shared with you. He confided in me on that memorable day that he was no longer going to stand by and just accept everything people told him. He made a conscious decision to ask more questions. One of those questions is "why?" So now instead of having a five-year-old grandson who asks why too much, I have a fifty-plus husband who has taken over. That day was almost ten years ago. Trust me when I say that I should now be calling my husband by the nickname YY. I've actually picked up the habit myself. I have asked myself a lot of why questions since that time and from that very same frame of reference.

The reason I felt the need to get ahead of myself today and start this chapter before I finished the last one is because I had a YY incident, which I felt everyone should hear about. While we were away down south, the people back home experienced a very cold winter. When we got back from our

140

southern abode, we soon discovered that we had a cracked glass panel in our front door unit. Frost was the culprit. This was not the first time it happened, but previously it was on a larger but less complicated window. At the time, we never bothered to make an insurance claim because the cost of replacement was less than our insurance deductible. This made perfect sense to us, and we never looked back. Once again, it crossed our minds that we might possibly do the same thing for this cracked window, but first we needed to do our homework and get an estimated cost for the repair. The first estimate was about twice as much as our deductible, so we decided to make an insurance claim. When we called our broker, he gave us a little "heads up," which we knew nothing about. He said that our insurance policy had an achievement clause. He went on to explain that because we were over fifty years old and hadn't made an insurance claim in over five years our deductible would be waived. We don't make insurance claims unless we absolutely have to, so little did he know that it was well over five years since we had made one.

Our broker then proceeded to contact our insurance company on our behalf. He then informed us that we would be receiving a call from an insurance adjustor to discuss the claim. When the representative called, he asked me to explain the situation directly to him. I told him about the glass breakage and the quote that we had received to repair the damage. As I explained earlier, the estimated cost came to double the amount of our deductible. This fellow was unaware that I knew about the achievement clause which was explained to us by our broker. When I told him about the potential cost, he quickly wanted to give me some advice. He went on to tell me that he felt it was better for us to just pay for all the repair costs of nearly a thousand dollars rather than make any claim at all. It had been his experience that it just wasn't worth it to make a claim because our insurance premiums would increase the following year, and we would regret it in the long run. I responded by asking him what the point of the insurance was in the first place. Here comes a Y question as you may very well have expected. Why have insurance if you're going to penalize us for using it? I explained that we never made a claim for our first broken window because it was below our deductible. Now he was suggesting we do the same thing and eat all the costs for the second one when it was double our deductible.

Some questions just begged to be asked. I then told him our age and that we hadn't had a claim in over five years. I informed him about the achievement clause. Guess what happened next? He said that he would look into it and phone me back. Sure enough he kept his word, and sure enough we qualified for a no deductible claim because of this clause. We managed to get our window repaired without paying a deductible and our premiums would not be going up because we checked that out too. By asking why, we got rewarded for being good customers instead of being penalized. Asking why is a good thing and it often times pays off in more than one way. When the insurance adjustor phoned back to inform me of the status of our claim, he was very professional. I have a sneaking suspicion that if he wasn't he knew I would ask why. "Success seems to be largely a matter of hanging on after others have let go."[137] Don't let go too soon. Ask all the pertinent questions that need to be asked before you give up. A little knowledge and persistence can pay off.

I want to share another cute little story with you. I actually read it in my doctor's office when I was there for an appointment. It was in one of those magazines that they leave around to busy ourselves with as we wait to get in to see the doctor. It was about a conversation that took place between a mother and her daughter. Every Sunday when they enjoyed a special meal of pot roast, the daughter noticed that before her mother put the roast into the oven, she would cut a slice off the top of the roast. Then she would lay this slice alongside the roast, put the lid on the roaster and stick it into the oven.

143

Finally, on one of these occasions, the daughter asked her mother why she did this. The mother answered that she didn't actually know the reason, but every time her mother prepared a roast she prepared it this way. This answer didn't satisfy the daughter, so her mother suggested she ask her grandmother in order to get the true explanation. The daughter thought that this was a good idea.

At the very next opportunity, she asked her grandmother to provide an explanation for following this procedure. Her grandmother did not know the answer either. All she could give her was the very same explanation that she had already heard from her own mother. Her mother always did it, and she just followed the same process with no questions asked. Fortunately, her elderly great grandmother was still living so the great granddaughter decided to ask her the now infamous question. The great grandmother explained that the reason she cut the slice off the roast was because she couldn't snugly fit the lid on the roaster. In other words, the roast was too big. However, even when the roast did fit, both the mother and the grandmother still continued to cut off a slice because neither one bothered to ask why it was being done in the first place.

How many times do we do things over and over again for no apparent reason and never ask why we are doing them?

This example is just an innocent, upbeat story to prove my point about the need to ask why more often. It certainly doesn't hurt to ask questions or to gather information about a situation that we aren't sure about. We could actually be engaging in some behavior in a repetitive way, which may be destructive to both our health and well-being. We could also be wasting time and energy on something that doesn't really need to be done. It's not to say that we want someone to roll their eyes at us because we are asking too many questions. It is only to say that when we need clarification, it is good to ask questions. It can pay off big time like it did for us with our insurance claim. A good bit of advice here, however, is to use a very respectful tone when dealing with people. I did with our insurance company, and that respect paid off. Once they did their own investigation into the achievement clause of our insurance policy, they behaved in a very professional way, much the same way I did. "Few things are impossible to diligence and skill...great works are performed not by strength, but perseverance."[138] Although this was just a simple task and not necessarily a great work, the point I want to make here is that perseverance can pay off whether the task is big or small. If the situation is important to you then it is worth it to investigate all your options thoroughly. "The rewards for those who persevere far exceed the pain that

145

must precede the victory."[139] In the end, you will be victorious more often.

Step 12 ~ Do your homework. Ask Y more often than not if it's important to you and you want to know the answers. There are no dumb questions. Just watch your tone when you ask them. Remember Step 5 about choosing whether to be like Mister Sun or Mister Wind. Step 12 and Step 5 work wonders together! Also try to remember that knowledge is power. Don't be afraid to do your research. Learn something new on a regular basis to expand your mind.

I'm All Shook Up!

I must admit I'm pretty excited not only about the completion of this book but about the publication of my first book. After I came up with the title for it, *I'm Not Perfect and It's Okay (A Baker's Dozen)*, I decided to write my pointers in step form. There are thirteen points to coincide with thirteen items in a baker's dozen. I consider the points to be my recipe to better cope with life. On completion of my first book, I immediately started to write this one because I knew I had more to say and more pointers to share as discussed in the first chapter of this book. I called them the donut holes because they supplement the original baker's dozen. Well right about now I probably have created some of the most lopsided donuts you are ever going to have to digest. The holes to the donuts are pretty well the same size as the donut itself because I have managed to write another book about the same length as the first.

Once again, I hope that you have enjoyed reading it as much as I have enjoyed writing it. It has been written with a desire to share and to help others who are in need of it. I agree with Robert G. Ingersoll when he writes of his own creed. He states, "Happiness is the only good. The time to be happy is now. The place to be happy is here. The way to be happy is to make others so."[140] A few of my lifelong friends were asking me about my book, and one of them quizzed me as to *why* I would write a book. Actually, they were all very curious. They wanted to understand my reasons for embracing such an endeavor and for putting myself in such a vulnerable position. I can honestly say that I wrote these two books because they were meant to be written. I was given both the desire and the talent to write them, therefore, even though I had the choice whether to say yes or no, I could hear the *tap, tap*. I knew it wouldn't stop until I answered it. I must admit that it has been a lot of work, but it has also brought me untold pleasure. "When a man feels throbbing within him the power to do what he undertakes as well as it can possibly be done, this is happiness, this is success."[141]

My family has been a huge support and I've gotten such a kick out of my husband and my daughters. I never told them my plan of simply writing the whole book before I let them read it, yet somehow or other they knew. My husband kept asking me what chapter I was on and my daughter just asked me the same question the other day. My husband has seen and heard me pounding away at my now, "red hot keyboard" for the last several weeks. He seems as eager to read what I have written as I am to share it.

As usual, I want to share a little story with you as I wind up this final extra chapter. I probably read it somewhere in a doctor's office, and I am now putting it into my own words. It is the story about a very wealthy man who had only one son. He loved this son very, very much. The depth of his love was almost overwhelming. When his son predeceased him, the depth of his despair was even more overwhelming. During this man's lifetime he had been a great collector of art. He had many fine paintings and other works of art that were extremely valuable. When his son was alive, this only son had fancied himself as an artist and had dabbled in painting. One picture he had painted was a self-portrait. The father not only loved this painting, he also cherished it because of his great love for his only son. The father hung it ever so graciously alongside all his other wonderful works of art for all to see and enjoy.

Of course when the man himself died, he had a will. He wanted all his fine works of art to be auctioned off with special instructions to his lawyer about what to do with the proceeds. When the day of the auction arrived, the room was full of art collectors and curators eager to bid on all the valuable pieces that were being displayed. There was a hush in the room as the auctioneer took his place at the podium, as the auction was about to begin. The silence was almost deafening. According to the father's instructions as written in his will, the first painting to be auctioned off was what he considered to be the beautiful painting of his only son. All of the art collectors knew which paintings were of the most value and were quite eager to get on with the rest of the auction.

When this self-portrait went up first, the room was especially silent. Finally, one man standing at the back of the room started to bid on this painting, for "a strong passion for any object will ensure success, for the desire of the end will point out the means."[142] The room remained silent. No one else had a desire to bid on or purchase this particular work of art. They were all more interested in the other, more valuable pieces. The auctioneer said, "Sold to the man at the back." Then he proceeded to start packing up his things to get ready to leave the room. All the other collectors started to make a racket and demanded to know what was going on. The auctioneer explained to them that he was doing what he had been instructed to do by the deceased man's lawyer. According to the father's will, he had requested that his son's picture be auctioned off first. Whoever was the highest bidder on his son's self-portrait would get the rest of his collection thrown in. Wise father, don't you think? His son meant the world to him. In the final analysis, it was based on

150

the premise of buy the picture of his son and you get the rest thrown in.

Buying into this philosophy or this picture is not unlike what God offers each of us with Jesus his only Son. Buy this picture, and everything else of value goes with it. The only thing that needs to be done is to say "yes" to the gift of salvation and the rest will fall into place. After you say "yes," the rest comes so much easier. We have the God-given right to say "no" because we have been given the gift of free will, but we can also say "yes" and receive the gift of salvation. This gift of salvation gets thrown in once we accept Jesus into our hearts and embrace the responsibility for ourselves and our own actions. Jesus is our Savior who has never sinned but accepts and forgives us as sinners and loves each of us with an everlasting and unconditional love. Jesus, the great one, would never turn his back on anyone of us. He knows the true meaning of agony and suffering and he accepted the greatest pain on earth for you and me. We have every reason to be grateful for the noblest sacrifice one can make for another human being. Jesus gave his life to save ours. I want to share another cute little story I heard just the other day. It was about a man who died and went to heaven. Upon his arrival, along with his long time loyal friend, his dog, he noticed two doors. He proceeded to knock at the first door. Both he and his dog were thirsty after their long journey. When the door opened, he was told that he could come in but his dog could not join him. The man then decided to knock on the second door. Both he and his dog were welcomed in and given both food and water. To me, this is what heaven is all about…Jesus died for the salvation of humankind. He is not prepared to leave anybody out. He loves saint and sinner alike. Perhaps you have heard this expression before…in essence; a saint is only a sinner trying to be a one. We are all sinners to varying degrees. Not one of us is exempt from human frailties, flaws, faults, or foibles. If there is one thing we all have in common it is this fact. Therefore, please try to remember this quote by Winston Churchill because I believe it applies in all that we say and do. "The price of greatness is responsibility."[143] Jesus died for our sins and for victory over death. By accepting responsibility for our sinfulness and embracing Jesus in our lives, we too have victory over death. This victory is our gift for saying "yes."

I remember an instance not so long ago on completion of my first book when I shared the fact that I had written it with one of my lifelong friends. I told him this information via e-mail, and he wrote back and asked me if it was a comedy or a tragedy. I chuckled to myself and wrote back that it was a bit of both, but I actually considered it to be a victory. Yes, writing these two books has been a true victory. Sharing them with my family and my friends has added to that victory. Now having the opportunity to share this victory with the world is beyond words. How could I ever refuse such an opportunity? I have been asked, and I have said "yes." What are you being asked to do? What are you going to answer? Is it going to be yes or no? Just remember the words of David Schwartz, "All great achievements require time."[144] Also remember those of Henry Drummond, "You will find as you look back upon your life that the moments when you have lived, are the moments when you have done things in the spirit of love."[145] When I take the time to ponder on the words of all the great thinkers I have been exposed to over the years, I am so inspired by their love, their wisdom, their desire and their devotion to make this a better world. They have either left their mark or are still in the process of doing so. I want to be one of these people. I want to share my words and make a difference. Don't you?

Now you have the other thirteen steps to what I consider to be better life coping skills. Between the first book and the second one, that adds up to twenty-six pointers. I consider these twenty-six steps to be the ABCs of my faith. I can't honestly say if I have finished "shaking it off" in reference to the first chapter, but I can say this. I definitely am all "shook up" in terms of being excited about the completion of my second book. If or when I choose to write a third book, should I be inspired to do so, it will not have any more steps. It's not to say that I won't continue to use the famous quotes the way that I have in the past, but I don't think the ABCs of my faith can be added to or taken from anymore.

Once again I look forward to my husband and my family reading this book for the first time. I also look forward to sharing it with all of you who have been so gracious to hear me out again. I want to thank each and every one of you for making the time in your busy lives to spend a little of it with me. In my first book, my husband was teasing me about whether I was a "know-it-all or all knowing." I finally have the answer for him. I'm a know-it-all because "it's what you learn after you know it all that counts."[146] I must say that as I have written these two books, I still cannot believe how much I've learned along the way. You know what else I've realized? The more I learn, the more I recognize how little I actually know. There is so much to learn in life that we must always be on the learning curve no matter how old we are because old age is no excuse for ignorance. Never—and I mean never—close your mind to new and exciting experiences.

Every day, visit all the rooms in your house and discover something new on a daily basis. Try it; you just might like it. It has been said that, "A total commitment is paramount to reaching the ultimate performance."[147] In order to be all that we can be we need to commit ourselves to nothing less than we are capable of becoming. Also remember that "you always pass failure on the way to success."[148] Doing our best, no matter what we are doing, is the key. Therefore, I will end this thirteenth chapter with a few words from Vince Lombardi. He says, "The price of success is hard work, dedication to the job at hand, and the determination that whether we win or lose, we have applied the best of ourselves to the task at hand."[149] As far as I'm concerned, anyone who has given it their best can never be a loser or a failure because "only those who dare to fail greatly can ever achieve greatly."[150]

Step 13 ~ Get excited about what is happening in your life. "The word enthusiasm is derived from two Greek words...*en* and *theos*. When combined to form the Greek word for enthusiasm, the term is literally translated a *God in you*!"[151] If there is one thing that you may have noticed about me through everything I have shared with you, it is probably my desire to have a positive attitude and a good outlook on life. As we all know, when life hands us a lemon, the best solution is to make lemonade. Therefore on that note, I suggest these simple reminders. Always focus on the positive. Make a list of 10 things in your life that you are thankful for and add to this list every month.

Conclusion

"We don't change God's message, His message changes us."[152]

I must say that I have never felt so inspired to do something as I have been to write the two books, which I have now completed. I cannot tell you how honored I am to have been chosen to share this message with all of you, my dear readers. I have no idea why I have been chosen because, simply put, I'm no more special than any one of you. The only plausible reason I can come up with is that I said "yes" to the Divine Inspiration that exists in each and every one of us. It is this inspiration that has brought about this dream of mine about sharing my healing process with you. I must admit that I have never considered myself to be any more talented or gifted than anyone else. From my point of view, I am not great at anything, but I am pretty good at several things. I refer to myself as a "jack of all trades and master of none."

Not so long ago, at one of my book signings, a woman in her mid-forties stopped by to chat with my daughter and me. Several times people dropped by to chat or pick a candy from the bowl I had sitting on the table. Most of these people were not interested in buying any book; let alone mine. The assistant manager in charge of book signings warned me up front. She was being considerate and wanted to spare my feelings in case I never sold one book. Apparently, this happens quite often. Some people who stopped by were also being kind and considerate. They didn't want to walk right by without acknowledging our presence.

One particular fellow stopped and went through this very same process of chatting me up. He then proceeded to take a complimentary candy. He was one of those guys that is very easy to remember. This was a new experience for my daughter, and a few minutes before this fellow's arrival, she wanted to know what to expect. She had asked me earlier what sort of people she might encounter and what should she say or do. Ironically enough, as I was describing this particular fellow, there he was again. I was more than willing to answer all his same questions; although it was apparent to me that he was far more interested in the free candy than in my book. This was perfectly fine by me.

Others stopped by and wanted to discuss their own lives and enjoy the atmosphere of having a person to listen to them. The lady that I first mentioned at the beginning of this Conclusion seemed to be very drawn to my book. In truth, I would say she was more drawn to just chatting with us rather than actually buying a book. After some time, and much to my surprise and pleasure, she decided to make the purchase of the book she had been looking for along with a copy of mine as well. She said her farewells and off she went.

About an hour later, one of the store employees sought me out and said I had a telephone call from a customer. *Uh oh,* I thought, *what have I done now?* Believe it or not, that call was from this very woman. She went home and for one reason or another immediately started reading my book. She actually cried on the phone because she could relate so much to some of the things I had written, and she felt so moved to let me know. This woman really made my day because she was very open to receiving my message. Each person is a whole world to God, and in some way God was able to reach this particular woman through me. The message has not changed. The message is the same for this woman as it is for me. I have been changed by the Messenger, and now I share the message. I have a sneaking suspicion that this woman received the same message. Maybe the words that I was inspired to write were part of the message she needed to hear. Are you willing to do the same? The message has been the same since the beginning of time. Love God. "Love your neighbor…whatsoever you do to the least of your brothers that you do unto me."[153] There you have it. That's the

159

message plain and simple. Loving others is what God is asking us to do. By doing so, we are demonstrating our love for God. I think Lydia Maria Child has chosen her words wisely when she says, "The cure for all the ills and wrongs, the cares, the sorrows, and the crimes of humanity, all lie in that one word 'love'. It is the divine vitality that everywhere produces and restores life."[154]

Love...yes; the greatest of these is love. When we truly realize and accept that we are lovable, we learn to see others in this same light. Growing up isn't that painful after all and in the end we may find several reasons to actually like it!

Epilogue

Flashback

Almost thirty years ago, as I was standing before my second grade class, it felt as if my life was falling apart. Happily married with three young daughters, I suddenly felt this unbelievable sense of dread and despair. After days and weeks, this feeling would not lift. It evolved into a deep depression that I could not escape and I sought out medical advice. Medication seemed to be the answer, but it backfired on me. Rather than referring me to a specialist, my doctor chose to continue increasing the dosage of the anti-depressant that he had initially prescribed.

I went from being depressed into a manic state which I later discovered was a side effect of the prescribed drug. The out of control "euphoria" was more than I could handle. Unable to sleep, I thought I was having the most incredible spiritual experience. I would flip back and forth between despair and mania. I had no idea what I was dealing with or what to do about the inner turmoil I was experiencing. It was at this time that I chose to seek out spiritual advice. After years of being a staunch Roman Catholic, I was shunned by a priest who had known me almost my entire life. In his ignorance about the reason for my confused state, he told me in no uncertain terms that "I'd better reconcile myself to God". In my condition, he might as well have told me to jump off a bridge.

In both my youth and my innocence, it never entered my mind that I was having an adverse reaction to my medication. Thirty years ago there were no television commercials warning what possible side effects to look for in prescription drugs nor were there cautionary warnings by my doctor. The negative side effects that I experienced were unbelievably painful and even more debilitating than the depression itself. If this makes any sense, I thought of suicide but I was not suicidal. In those days, you trusted what your doctor said. I trusted mine. In those days, you also trusted what the priests said. I trusted that priest too by reaching out to him for guidance. Both of these men let me down and I suffered the consequences of it. Now I had no idea what to do or who to turn to, to get the help that I so desperately needed. Therefore, I did the only thing I could think of in this indescribable state. I got on my hands and knees and prayed like I had never prayed before in my whole life. I sought out the peace and comfort of a loving and forgiving God. At the depths of my despair, I found a renewed faith in a merciful God. I revisited my childhood education and I questioned some of the teachings. In doing so, I was able to face the reasons for my serious depression. I thought I was being punished but I wasn't sure why. With time, I was able to work through the guilt that I was feeling and I learned to actually accept the unconditional love of my Creator.

I never truly knew the meaning of faith until I was so filled with fear. It was then that God reached out His hand and saved me from the depths of confusion and despair. This powerful experience is one I will never forget. It is very difficult to describe the healing balm of the Holy Spirit that I received during this critical time in my life. For that, I will be forever grateful. I ended up with more faith and trust in My Maker than I could ever have imagined. Now that I have put this message into words, my healing circle is complete. I sincerely hope that you can learn from my experiences and find your healing circle too. I have discovered that what appears to be the end may really be a new beginning. My books, *I'm Not Perfect and It's Okay* and *Growing Up and Liking It*, are proof of it!

"I am a little pencil in the hand of a writing God who is sending a love letter to the world." [155]

Sample Chapter from ~ Up The "Down" Ladder (Simple Ideas to Overcome Depression)

1 ~ Little Things

"It is not the straining for great things that is most effective; it is doing the little things, the common duties, a little better and better" ~ Elizabeth Stuart Phelps

Do you feel like you are in a rut? How many of us look at our lives and feel inadequate, insecure and unfulfilled? I'm still surprised when I hear people talk about these kinds of emotions and how alone they feel. "Instead of suppressing conflicts, specific channels could be created to make the conflict explicit, and specific methods could be set up by which the conflict is resolved." (Wynn Davis) In our culture, negative feelings are far more common than not. You are not unique, nor permanently scarred because you have such feelings. It's just that most people may prefer to hide what they are experiencing because they see it as a form of weakness and they don't want anyone to know or capitalize on it. At times, this may appear to be a very good strategy; however, to think that we are the only ones who struggle with negative thoughts and feelings, is only doing an injustice and disservice to ourselves. "We must become acquainted with our emotional household; we must see our feelings as they actually are. This breaks their hypnotic and damaging hold on us." (Vernon Howard) It is far more beneficial to embrace our negative cycles in life and admit that we could use a boost to our self-esteem.

At the beginning of this self-help book, I would like to make my point very clear. I want to stress that I am talking about what I consider to be "normal" down or negative cycles in life. You know, the times when nothing seems to be going our way and we just can't seem to do a thing right. Believe it or not, most of us have these experiences at one time or another. This is the kind of rut I asked you about in the first paragraph of this chapter. "Experience has taught me this, that we undo ourselves by impatience. Misfortunes have their life and their limits, their sickness and their health." (Michel Eyquem De Montaigne) The negatives that we experience in life usually do not last forever. Life has many up and downs and learning to effectively deal with life's challenges is the only way to find the joy we are all seeking in this world we call home. If you are not happy with your life and you feel in a rut, instead of just spinning your back wheels, it is wiser to make some smaller life altering changes in order to get out of your negative situation.

First of all, we must ask and answer a few pertinent questions. For instance, is it your job that is causing you grief? Is it your home situation whether with your spouse or your children? Has it got to do with other family members or friends? What I'm suggesting here is that you have a little honest question and answer period with yourself. Perhaps, the best course of action is to merely answer these questions with a simple yes or no. I can ask you all kinds of questions to give you food for thought but I can't get inside your head to hear the answers. Only you can do that. In other words, it is necessary to do a little self-analysis. I am well aware that not all answers are as cut and dry as a yes or no but it's a start. It may help decipher the real problem areas in your life in order to help focus on the areas that require the most attention.

My daughter mentioned that the first book I wrote was far more appealing to my generation than to hers. She was right. Most of the feedback I have received is from the people of my era. They can really relate to a lot of my experiences because they've lived through many of them and quickly related to what I meant and the life lessons I learned.

Ironically enough, what strikes one person as pertinent information, may be totally irrelevant to another. I find it very interesting and somewhat challenging to come up with some answers to the questions posed while trying to consider the needs of each individual. This is especially challenging when it is necessary to compose the questions in order to figure out where this younger generation might be coming from and what they would like to know. I sense that they have every desire to solve their problems but in all honesty part of the challenge for them is recognizing what the problems are so that they can better resolve them. However, I will say this. One of my observations when looking at this generation (30 something), is their need to compare or compete. These two words are not necessarily synonymous, but at times, are confused by the parties involved. One of the questions that keeps popping into my mind and for good reason is this, "How do you reduce the feelings of comparing the workloads of each spouse and how do you reduce feeling competitive about it?" I was actually asked this particular question therefore; I am going to make every effort to answer it by distinguishing between the differences of comparing ourselves to our spouses and being competitive with them.

"We can chart our future clearly and wisely only when we know the path which has led to the present." (Adlai

Stevenson) . We all know that it isn't easy to ask for advice and it's even harder to actually act on it especially when it's coming from our parents. This concept in itself is an age old mystery. Even adult children usually prefer to learn from their own mistakes or from other sources rather than learn from ours, as their parents. I think at some level, this is a subtle form of rebellion that takes well into adult life before it is recognized and eventually overcome. Embracing this concept may very well enhance the process of getting up the "down" ladder.

When figuring out how to address the question about reducing feelings of comparison and competitiveness, the initial thing that popped into my mind was the story we used to read to our children when they were young. Perhaps, you can recall too. The title is Goofy and His Wife. I will get back to that story at the end of this chapter. For now, I want to address the fact that I have noticed this need to compare workloads amongst many young married couples. According to my experience, this was not a problem with my peers in our child raising years. Therefore, it is necessary to address this question from my frame of reference in order to figure out what changed. In doing so, it will provide a better understanding of how to arrive at a solution. "Life…can only be understood backwards…" (Soren Kierkegard)

In my opinion, as time unfolds and evolves, societal values may change. When I look back at my own childhood, a mother working outside the home was almost nonexistent. At least, this was the case with my own peers. Later on, as my generation became adults, it became apparent that mothers were not as satisfied with staying home because they were attaining more education and desired more equality, monetary benefits, independence, status, and so on. When men were the primary bread earners, the roles were very clearly defined. As the woman's role changed these lines became smudged. Women came to realize that mothers are nowhere nearly as highly regarded as their counterparts in the work force. It would seem that this is when the battle of the wills or perhaps battle of the sexes started to set in. When you are a stay-at-home mother you may be inadvertently regarded as less than a working mother outside the home. This view may be held by some members of society including women themselves. Over the years, as women strive for more equality, this imbalance does not sit well with them. Usually, when women are in the workforce, either out of necessity or desire, they have a better sense of self-esteem or personal accomplishment because their efforts are rewarded. On the other hand, stay-at-home mothers have no reward system set up for them and therefore, at times it may seem like a thankless job.

The only way to actually reduce what I'm thinking are negative feelings, is to honestly admit exactly what you are experiencing. "There's no feeling quite like the one you get when you get to the truth: You're the captain of the ship called you. You're setting the course, the speed, and you're out there on the bridge, steering." (Carl Frederick) Although, a healthy competitiveness can exist between spouses, there can also be an unhealthy resentment if it is stemming from negative emotions. So let's start here. Remember for every problem there is a solution. "Each problem has hidden in it an opportunity so powerful that it literally dwarfs the problem. The greatest success stories were created by people who recognized a problem and turned it into an opportunity." (Joseph Sugarman)

Okay...so what feelings are we really dealing with and where do we go from here?

In essence, you as younger wives and mothers are "in the moment". I am looking back while you are presently experiencing the types of frustration that most young mothers today can identify with...and are searching for suggestions and possible solutions for this dilemma. I think most mothers want to enjoy their young children at this stage of life instead of wishing these years away in order to experience more personal freedom and flexibility in their own lives. The main concern seems to be the imbalance in the relationship between the husband and wife and the sharing of family duties. There is a third aspect to be considered when it comes to the imbalance that may occur in a family household. At times, children can also disrupt the balance that parents might be trying to establish in the family home, by having some of their own needs and demands. I believe it is necessary to keep this in mind while I discuss the differences between comparing and competing with our spouses. I think raising a family contributes and adds to the stresses of life which may result in the need to compare. I don't sense much competition in this scenario. It is far more about comparing the workloads and experiencing frustration and anger if we think we are carrying more than our fair share of the load.

Now, I feel the need to return to the story of Goofy and His Wife in order to make some necessary points as far as comparing our lives to our spouses. I enjoyed reading this particular book because I could identify with it. I am still smiling as I remember this story so well. As far as I'm concerned this is a "must read" for all young families. It seems to capture so much wisdom in such a simple little childhood book. In this story, it is actually Goofy, the husband who isn't happy with the workload in his life. He feels that his wife is not carrying her fair share of the load and he would like this situation remedied. Due to the fact that she stays at home, Goofy doesn't see his wife as actually working as hard as he does. He may come from that old school of thought that existed in my era. The old notion of, if you're not earning money...than you are not really working. Has this idea really evolved as much as we would like to believe? At times, I'm not so sure it has or at least, I haven't seen as much proof as I would like to see.

Now, getting back to Goofy, at his insistence, he and his wife agreed to swap roles in order to evaluate if their individual roles in the family were fair and equitable. Although, Goofy's wife went off to work and took over his job, in this book we only get to see how Goofy's life unfolded on the first day in his new job as homemaker. I was very amused as Goofy flubbed time after time in his efforts to get all the household chores done. By the time his wife returned home from work, he was so relieved to see her and eagerly wanted to go back to his old life. After this initial job switch, he had a new understanding of his wife's workload and a new found respect and appreciation for her as well. In all fairness, we never did see how Goofy's wife fared in her first day at

Goofy's job. The reason for Goofy's day being the focus of this book is probably because he was the one doing the griping. At times, we can all complain about the stress we experience in life because of what we see as unfair. It doesn't only happen between spouses, it happens in the workplace over and over again. For one reason or another, this personality trait seems to have a common thread that weaves its way through many aspects of our lives.

The more we compare, the more we think we are doing and the less we think our counterparts are doing. It's this constant need to compare that ends up causing so much resentment and subsequent grief as we see our spouses coming up short in regard to our expectations of them. This is the reason I think the root of the problem is far more about comparing and dealing with feelings of resentment, rather than having a natural competitiveness that may exist in other relationships. Comparing ourselves to others in any situation including marriage has little or no positive end results. On the other hand, a healthy competitiveness can have its benefits as it encourages us to strive for higher goals and better results as we try to emulate those that we admire and respect. "There is one quality which one must possess to win, and that is definiteness of purpose, the knowledge of what one wants, and a burning desire to possess it." (Napoleon Hill)

When we reach these goals, we usually experience a better sense of self, accompanied with more confidence and self-esteem. In other words, healthy competition is good; however, comparing our workloads to others is actually negative and seldom makes us feel good. It's like using some kind of invisible measuring tool. When we see ourselves as doing more or having less than other people including our partners, it only serves to anger us and builds resentment. In most instances, these negative emotions reduce our confidence and self-esteem. In essence when we compare ourselves to others, it can have the exact opposite effect. Instead of feeling good about ourselves, we end up feeling worse. It's a no win situation.

I think the reason for so much comparison may lie in how the job of homemaker is viewed by the individual or even by society at large. Being a mother/homemaker and engaging in all the mundane tasks (wiping runny noses, changing soiled diapers, housecleaning, etc.) that go with this role in life are not necessarily highly regarded by others including ourselves. Perhaps it is necessary to give this type of work a better image, a higher job rating, more benefits, and more compensation...not necessarily in the monetary form but that wouldn't hurt either! The main way to reduce negative feelings is to realize what is causing them in the first place. My point is that it is wise to concentrate on your own role in life and your attitude about it. There is only one person that you can change in this world and that is yourself. Love what you do and everyone will want your job. The quote below makes perfect sense to me. How about you?

"Put the uncommon effort into the common task… make it large by doing it in a great way." ~ Orison Swett Marden

TO CONTACT AUTHOR:

WEBSITE

http://www.doloresayotte.com

BLOG SITE

http://www.doloresayotte.wordpress.com

FACEBOOK AUTHOR'S PAGE

http://www.facebook.com/Author.Dolores.Ayotte

Bibliography

"Charles Poore quotes." Thinkexist.com,
http://thinkexist.com/quotes/charles_poore/. (Accessed October 12, 2008).

"Author Unknown." Religious One Liners. http://www.joe-
ks.com/archives_feb2007/Religious_One_Liners.htm (Accessed February
22, 2009).

"Author Unknown." Talk Jesus. http://www.talkjesus.com/lounge/6828-
will-god-will-never-take-you.html (Accessed February 22, 2009).

"Ralph Waldo Emerson quotes." About.com:Quotations.
http://quotations.about.com/od/stillmorefamouspeople/a/RalphWaldoEme
r7.htm (Accessed February 22, 2009).

"Thomas Jefferson quotes." Quoteworld.org.
http://www.quoteworld.org/quotes/7147 (Accessed October 12, 2008).

"James Agee quotes." Quoteworld.org.
http://www.quoteworld.org/quotes/233 (Accessed October 12, 2008).

"Demosthenes quotes." The Quotation Page.
http://www.quotationspage.com/quote/29680.html (Accessed October 12,
2008).

"Vincent T. Lombardi quotes." Quoteworld.org.
http://www.quoteworld.org/quotes/8402 (Accessed October 12, 2008).

"Bernard Edmond quotes." Quoteworld.org.
http://www.quoteworld.org/quotes/4004. (Accessed October 12, 2008).

"Vincent T. Lombardi quotes." Quoteworld.org.
http://www.quoteworld.org/quotes/8403 (Accessed October 12, 2008).

"Scott Reed quotes." Quoteland.com.
http://www.quoteland.com/author.asp?AUTHOR_ID=621 (Accessed
October 29, 2008).

"Napoleon Hill quotes." BrainyQuote.
http://www.brainyquote.com/quotes/authors/n/napoleon_hill.html
(Accessed October 29, 2008).

"George Bernard Shaw quotes." QuoteDB.
http://www.quotedb.com/quotes/932 (Accessed October 29, 2008).

"Abraham Lincoln quotes." quoteworld.org.
http://www.quoteworld.prg/quotes/10282 (Accessed October 29, 2008).

"Claude M. Bristol quotes." Thinkexist.com.
http://thinkexist.com/quotes/claude_m_bristol/ (Accessed October 29,
2008).

"Elbert Hubbard quotes." QuotationsBook.
http://quotationsbook.com/quote/26725/ (Accessed October 29, 2008).

"Dale Carnegie quotes." BrainyQuote.
http://www.brainyquote.com/quotes/authors/d/dale_carnegie.html
(Accessed October 29, 2008).

"John McDonald quotes." QuotationsBook.
http://quotationsbook.com/quote/10618/ (Accessed October 29, 2008).
"Eric Hoffer quotes." BrainyQuote.
http://www.brainyquote.com/quotes/authors/e/eric_hoffer.html (Accessed October 29, 2008).
"Leo Buscaglia quotes." Hungrybear Blog. ScrapSayings, Love and Marriage. http://scrapsayings.com/say-love.htm (Accessed October 11, 2009).
"Michael Korda quotes." Thinkexist.com.
http://thinkexist.com/quotes/michael_korda/ (Accessed October 27, 2008).
" Whitney Griswold quotes." Eugene C. Gerhart, Quote It Completely (Buffalo, New York: Wm.S.Hein Publishing, 1998).
"John D. Rockefeller quotes." the painter's key.
http://quote.robertgenn.com/getquotes.php?catid=1 (Accessed October 27, 2008).
"Henry Ward Beecher quotes." BrainyQuote.
http://www.brainyquote.com/quotes/authors/h/henry_ward_beesher.html (Accessed October 27, 2008).
"Author Unknown. " BellaOnline: The Voice of Women.
http://www.bellaonline.com/articles/art41795.asp (Accessed October 23, 2008).
(Accessed October 21, 2008).
"Tyron Edwards quotes." Thinkexist.com.
http://thinkexist.com/quotes/with/keyword/dagger/ (Accessed October 21, 2008).
"Albert Pine quotes." Thinkexist.com.
http://thinkexist.com/quotes/albert_pine/ (Accessed October 22, 2008).
"John Wanamaker quotes." Quote Lady's Quotes.
http://www.quotelady.com/subjects/thankfulness.html (Accessed October 11, 2009).
"Pearl Bailey quotes." BrainyQuote.
http://www.brainyquote.com/quotes/authors/p/pearl_bailey.html (Accessed October 22, 2008).
"Napoleon Hill quotes." BrainyQuote.
http://www.brainyquote.com/quotes/authors/n/napoleon_hill.html (Accessed October 22, 2008).
"Andy Rooney quotes." My Favorite Ezines.
http://www.myfavoriteezines.com/ezinedirectory/quotes-about-aging-elderly.html (Accessed October 22, 2008).
August T. Jaccaci and Susan B. Gault, 2000, CEO – Chief Evolutionary Officer, (Woburn, MA: Butterworth & Heinemann, 1999).
"Andy Rooney Quotes." wowzone.
http://www.wowzone.com/rooney.html (Accessed October 22, 2008).

"Peter 3:4." Beauty & Being Beautiful Christian Advice. http://www.christianadvice.net/about_beauty.htm (Accessed October 22, 2008).

"George MacDonald quotes." WorldofQuotes.com. http://www.worldofquotes.com/topic/Help/1/index.html (Accessed October 22, 2008).

"W. Somerset Maugham quotes." BrainyQuote. http://www.brainyquote.com/quotes/authors/w/w_somerset_maugham.ht ml (Accessed October 23, 2008).

"Peter Nivio Zarlenga quotes." Quoteland.com. http://www.quoteland.com/author.asp?AUTHOR_ID=636 (Accessed October 23, 2008).

"Francois De La Rochefoucauld quotes." BrainyQuote. http://www.brainyquote.com/quotes/authors/f/framcois_de_la_rochefouca.h tml (Accessed October 23, 2008).

"Andy Rooney quote." goodreads. http://www.goodreads.com/quotes/show/132234 (Accessed October 23, 2008).

"Josh Billings quotes." Happen-quotes. http://happenstance-music.com/quotes-all.asp (Accessed October 23, 2008).

"Alexander Graham Bell quotes." Wynn Davis, The Best of Success (Lombard, Illinois: Successories Publishing, 1992).

"Booker T. Washington quotes." QuoteDB. http://quotedb.com/authors/booker-t-washington (Accessed October 23, 2008).

"Ralph Waldo Emerson quotes." PBBA Atlantic Inc. http://www.pbbaatlantic.com/Default.asp?Page=380 (Accessed October 23, 2008).

"Richard Bach quotes." BrainyQuote. http://www.brainyquote.com/quotes/authors/r/richard_bach.html (Accessed October 23, 2008).

"Ben Stein quotes." Thinkexist.com. http://thinkexist.com/quotes/ben_stein/ (Accessed October 23, 2008).

"Author Unknown." QuotationsBook. http://quotationsbook.com/quote/27210/ (Accessed October 23, 2008).

"George Bernard Shaw quotes." BrainyQuote. http://www.brainyquote.com/quotes/authors/g/george_bernard_shaw.html (Accessed October 23, 2008).

"B.C. Forbes quotes." BrainyQuote. http://www.brainyquote.com/quotes/authors/b/b_c_forbes.html (Accessed October 23, 2008).

"Jack Youngblood quotes." BrainyQuote.
http://www.brainyquote.com/quotes/authors/j/jack_youngblood.html
(Accessed October 18, 2008).
"John Norley quotes." World of Quotes.com.
http://www.worldofquotes.com/author/John-Norley/i/index.html
(Accessed October 18, 2008).
"Josh Billings quotes." BrainyQuote.
http://www.brainyquote.com/quotes/quotes/j/joshbillin161323.html
(Accessed October 18, 2008).
Mac Lucado, Six Hours One Friday: Living In The Power Of The Cross
(Nashville, Tennessee, Thomas Nelson Inc. 1989 & 2004).
"Thomas Carlyle quotes." BrainyQuote.
http://www.brainyquote/quotes/authors/t/thomas_carlyle.html (Accessed
October 18, 2008).
"Don Herold quotes." World of Quotes.com.
http://www.worldofquotes/topic/Morality/i/index.html (Accessed October
18, 2008).
"Dwight D. Moody quotes." Bob Kelly, Worth Reading (Grand Rapids,
Michigan: Kregel Publications, 2003).
"Louisa May Alcott quotes." About.com. (Women's History).
http://womenshistory.about.com/cs/quotes/a/qu_lm_alcott.html (Accessed
October 18, 2008).
"Jane Ellice Hopkins quotes." Said What.
http://www.saidwhat.com/quotes/favourite/jane_ellice_hopkins
(Accessed October 18, 2008).
"Francis Bacon quotes." BrainyQuote.
http://www.brainyquote.com/quotes/authors/f/francis_bacon.html
(Accessed October 18, 2008).
"Thomas Moore quotes." Empyrean Friendship Quotes.
http://www.empyrean.ca/words/quotes/friends.html (Accessed October
18, 2008).
Patricia Covalt PhD, What Smart Couples Know (New York, NY:
Amacom, August, 2007).
"David Starr Jordan quotes." Thinkexist.com.
http://www.thinkexist.com/quotation/wisdom_is_knowing_what_to_do_n
ext-skill_is/253363.html (Accessed October 18, 2008).
"Martha Washington quotes." The Quotations Page.
http://www.quotationspage.com/quote/Martha_Washington/ (Accessed
October 18, 2008).
"William James quotes." BrainyQuote.
http://www.brainyquote.com/quotes/quotes/w/williamjam163783.html
(Accessed October 18, 2008).

"Joseph Marmion quotes." Christianbook.com.
http://www.christianbook.com/Christian/Book/product?item_no=722100
&event=cfn (Accessed October 19, 2008).
"Marie Curie quotes." The Quotations Page.
http://www.quotationspage.com/quote/34023.html (Accessed October 19,
2008).
"Robert Schuller quotes." fusioncoaching!
http://www.fusioncoaching.net/quotes.asp (Accessed October 19, 2008).
"Ben Stein quotes." refdeask.com. http://www.refdesk.com/nov01td.html
(Accessed October 19, 2008).
"George Bernard Shaw quotes." Sententiae.org.
http://www.sententiae.org/node/67317 (Accessed October 19, 2008).
"Norman Dowty quotes." xanga (jmejo327 weblog).
http://www.weblog.xanga.com/jmejo327/616206831/item.html?page=1&
jump=1373497756&leftcmt=1#1373497756 (Accessed October 19,
2008).
"Jose Bergamin quotes." BrainyQuote.
http://www,brainyquote.com/quotes/authors/j/jose_bergamin.html
(Accessed October 19, 2008).
"Clarence Smithson quotes." My Favorite Ezines.
http://www.myfavoriteezines.com/ezinedirectory/quotes-about-faith.html
(Accessed October 19, 2008).
"Doris Leasing quotes." quoteworld.org.
http://www.quoteworld.org/quotes/8217 (Accessed October 19, 2008).
"Daniel H. Burnham quotes." WorldofQuotes.com.
http://www.worldofquotes.com/author/Daniel-H-Burnham/1/index.html
(Accessed October 19, 2008).
"Jean Paul Satre quotes." WorldofQuotes.com.
http://www.worldofquotes.com/topic/Freedom/1/index.html (Accessed
October 19, 2008).
"Ralph Waldo Emerson quotes." The Quote Garden.
http://www.quotegarden.com/graduation.html (Accessed October 19,
2008).
"Alan Alda quotes." Flickr.
http://www.flickr.com/photo/journey/tonowhere/190154806/ (Accessed
October 20, 2008).
"Seneca quotes." HighBeam Research.
http://www.highbeam.com/doc/1G1-177290627.html (Accessed October
20, 2008).
"George Patton quotes." QuoteDB. http://www.quotedb.com/quotes/2092
(Accessed October 20, 2008).

"William Penn quotes." BrainyQuote.
http://www.brainyquote.com/quotes/authors/w/william_penn.html
(Accessed October 20, 2008).
"William Jennings quotes." quoteworld.org.
http://www.quoteworld.org/quotes/2011 (Accessed October 20, 2008).
"Louis Pasteur quotes." QuoteDB. http://www.quotedb.com/quotes/2195
(Accessed October 20, 2008).
"John Ruskin quotes." BrainyQuote.
http://www.brainyquote.com/quotes/quotes/j/johnruskin135097.html
(Accessed October 20, 2008).
"George Bernard Shaw quotes." The Quotations Page.
http://www.quotationspage.com/quotes/George_Bernard_Shaw/31
(Accessed October 20, 2008).
"English Proverb." PROVERBS AND ENGLISH SAYINGS.
http://www.english-sayings.com/the-hand-that-gives-gathers/4638
(Accessed October 20, 2008).
"Bob Richards quotes." BrainyQuote.
http://www.braintquote.com/quotes/authors/b/bob_richards.html
(Accessed October 20, 2008).
"Ralph Waldo Emerson quotes." The Quotations Page.
http://www.quotationspage.com/quote/2070.html (Accessed October 20,
2008).
"Dr. Albert Schweitzer quotes." The Quotations Page.
http://www.quotationspage.com/quote/4120.html (Accessed October 20,
2008).
"Author Unknown." The Positivity Blog.
http://www.positivityblog.com/indexphp/2007/04/30/20-inpirational -
quotes-on-happiness/ (Accessed October 26, 2008).
"Arnold Toynbee quotes." Thinkexist.com.
http://thinkexist.com/quotes/arnold_toynbee/ (Accessed October 26,
2008).
"Flora Edwards quotes." Thinkexist.com.
http://thinkexist.com/quotes/flora_edwards/ (Accessed October 26, 2008).
"George Santayana quotes." The Quotations Page.
http://www.quotationspage.com/quotes/George_Santayana (Accessed
October 26, 2008).
"Horace quotes." The Quotations Page.
http://www.quotationspage.com/quotes/2954.html (Accessed October 26,
2008).
"Robert J. Mckain quotes." Thinkexist.com.
http://thinkexist.com/quotes/robert_j_mckain/ (Accessed October 26,
2008).

"Dwight L. Moody quotes." What Quote.
http://www.whatquote.com/quotes/Dwight_L_Moody/14241-Faith-makes-all-thin.html (Accessed October 26, 2008).

"Phillips Brooks quotes." Wikiquote.
http://en.wikiquote.org/wiki/Phillips_Brooks (Accessed October 26, 2008).

"Marcus Aurelius quotes." BrainyQuote.
http://www.brainyquote.com/quotes/quoyes/m/marcusaure10790.html (Accessed October 26, 2008).

"Confucius quotes." Thinkexist.com.
http://thinkexist.com/quotations/study_without_reflection_is_a_waste_of_time/170664.html (Accessed October 26, 2008).

"Paul G. Thomas quotes." DictionaryQuotes.
http://www.dictionaryquotes.com/authorquotations/2873/Paul_G_Thomas.php (Accessed October 26, 2008).

"James Allen quotes." BrainyQuote.
http://www.brainyquote.com/quotes/authors/j/james_allen.html (Accessed October 26, 2008).

"Albert Einstein quotes." QuotationsBook.
http://quotationsbook.com/quote/19649/ (Accessed October 26, 2008).

"Thomas Merton quotes." Thinkexist.com.
http://thinkexist.com/quotes/thomas_merton/ (Accessed October 26, 2008).

"Ambrose Bierce quotes. BrainyQuote.
http://www.brainyquote.com/quotes/authors/a/ambrose_bierce.html (Accessed October 26, 2008).

"Bernard M. Baruch quotes." Famous Inspirational Quotes.
http://www.inspirationalquotes4u.com/baruchquotes/index.html (Accessed October 26, 2008).

"James A. Michener quotes." BrainyQuote.
http://www.brainyquote.com/quotes/authors/j/james_a_michener.html (Accessed October 26, 2008).

"H. Stanley Judd quotes." BrainyQuote.
http://www.brainyquote.com/quotes/authors/h/h_stanley_judd.html (Accessed October 26, 2008).

"Robert Louis Stevenson quotes." BrainyQuote.
http://www.brainyquote.com/quotes/authors/r/robert_louis_stevenson.html (Accessed October 26, 2008).

"Thomas Carlyle quotes." BrainyQuote.
http://www.brainyquote.com/quotes/authors/t/thomascarl118220.html (Accessed October 26, 2008).

"Washington Irving quotes." GIGA Quotes. http://www.giga-usa.com/quotes/authors/washington_irving_a001.html (Accessed October 26, 2008).

"Ralph Waldo Emerson quotes." Quotes and Poem.com. http://www.quotesandpoem.com/quotes/showquotes/subject/Perseverance /4923 (Accessed October 26, 2008).

"Orison Swett Marden quotes." BrainyQuote. http://www.brainyquote.com/quotes/authors/o/orison_swett_marden.html (Accessed October 26, 2008).

"Libbie Fudium quotes." QuoteMountain.com. http://quotemountain.org/sayings/scrapbook_sayings/ (Accessed October 15, 2008).

"Albert Camus quotes." Allgreat Quotes. http://www.allgreatquotes.com/friendship_quotes12.html (Accessed October 15, 2008).

"C. S. Lewis quotes." Thinkexist.com. http:///www.thinkexist.com/every_day_in_a_life_fills_the_whole_life_wi th/345885.html (Accessed October 15, 2008).

"Gloria Gaither quotes." Reflections of Moi blog. http://www.reflectionsofmoiblogspot.com/2007/11/there_is_smothing_in _every_season_in.html (Accessed October 15, 2008).

"J.M. Triggs quotes." Carpe Diem Sermon, October 17, 1996. http://biblestudy.churches.net/base/SEIZE.TXT (Accessed October 15, 2008).

"Author Unknown." The Board of Wisdom. http://www.boardofwisdom.com/mailquote.asp?msgid=38056 (Accessed October 15, 2008).

"Plutarch quotes." Quotes about God, http://www.wow4u.com/qgod/index.html (Accessed October 11, 2009).

"Author Unknown." Angelfire. http://angelfire.com/mi/peachpenguin/quotes/friend.html (Accessed October 15, 2008).

"Arnold Glasow quotes." Thinkexist.com. http://thinkexist.com/quotes/arnold_h._glasgow/3.html (Accessed October 10, 2009).

"Heabar quotes." Redbubble. http://www.redbubble.com/search/gardener%20sunset?&page=3 (Accessed October 15, 2008).

"Author Unknown." Country Heart Designs. http:/www.countryheartdesigns.com/friendship.html (Accessed October 15, 2008).

"Abraham Lincoln quotes." Quoteworld.org. www://quoteworld.org/quotes/8336 (Accessed October 15, 2008).

"Johnny Cash quotes." Words of Inspiration.
http://www.public.asu.edu/~cyndee74/inspire.htm (Accessed October 15, 2008).

"Orison Swett Marden quotes." Quote Cosmos.
http://www.quotecosmos.com/quotes/8142view (Accessed October 15, 2008).

"Thomas Merton quotes." UBR, Inc. http://www.quotes.ubr.com/quotes-alphabetical/h-quotes/happiness-quotes.aspx. (Accessed October 15, 2008).

"James Keller quotes." cybernation.com.
http://www.cybernation.com/quotationcenter/quoteshow.php?id123 (Accessed October 15, 2008).

"Hellen Keller quotes." MANGERS FORUM.
http://managersforum.com/Quotes/QuoteDetail.asp?Type=FEAR (Accessed October 15, 2008).

"Eleanor Roosevelt quotes." The Quotation Page.
http://quotationspage.com/quote/26369.html (Accessed October 15, 2008).

"William Feathers quotes." BrainyQuote.
http://www.brainyquote.com/quotes/authors/w/william_feathers.html (Accessed October 24, 2008).

"Samuel Johnson quotes." The Quotations Page.
http://www.quotationspage.com/quotes/Samuel_Johnson (Accessed October 24, 2008).

"Ted W. Engstrom quotes." quotewold.org.
http://www.quoteworld.org/authors/ted_w_engstrom (Accessed October 24, 2008).

"Robert G. Ingersoll quotes." QuotationsBook.
http://quotationsbook.com/quote/18384/ (Accessed October 30, 2008).

"Orison Swett Marden quotes." Thinkexist.com.
http://thinkexist.com/quotes/with/keyword/throbbing/ (Accessed October 30, 2008).

"William Hazlitt quotes." QuotationsBook.
http://quotationsbook.com/quote/10590/ (Accessed October 30, 2008).

"Winston Churchill quotes." QuoteDB.
http://www.quotedb.com/quotes/1039 (Accessed October 30, 2008).

"David J. Schwartz quotes." QuotationsBook.
http://quotationsbook.com/quote/30047/ (Accessed October 30, 2008).

"Henry Drummond quotes." BrainyQuote.
http://www.brainyquoye.com/quotes/authors/h/henry_drummond.html (Accessed October 30, 2008).

"John Wooden quotes." BrainyQuote.
http://www.brainyquote.com/quotes/authors/j/john_wooden.html
(Accessed October 30, 2008).
"Tom Flores quotes." WorldofQuotes.com.
http://www.worldofquotes.com/authors/Tom_Flores/1/index.html
(Accessed October 30, 2008).
"Mickey Rooney quotes." The Quotation Page.
http://www.quotationspage.com/quote/1627.html (Accessed October 30,
2008).
"Vince Lombardi quotes." Thinkexist.com.
http://thinkexist.com/quotes/vince_lombardi/ (Accessed October 30,
2008).
"Robert Kennedy quotes." QuoteDB.
http://www.quotedb.com/quotes/2713 (Accessed October 30, 2008).
"L.D. Turner quotes." Lifebook International, Attitudes of Blessing:
Enthusiasm – February 26, 2008.
http://lifebook.wordpress.com/2008/02/26/attitudes-of-blessing-
enthusiasm/ (Accessed October 30, 2008).
"Author Unknown." Slideshare. http://www.slideshare.net/webtel/26-
beautiful-one-liners
 (Accessed February 22, 2009).
"Bible quotes." Salvation Economist Weblog, February 18, 2009.
http://salvationeconomist.wordpress.com/ (Accessed October 11, 2009).
"Lydia Maria Child quotes." About.com.
http://womenshistory.about.com/od/quotes/a/lm_child.htm (Accessed
October 30, 2008).
"Mother Teresa quotes," Thinkexist.com,
http://thinkexist.com/quotation/i_am_a_little_pencil_in_the_hand_of_a_
writing_god/215428.html (Accessed October 14, 2010).

Endnotes

[1] "Charles Poore quotes," Thinkexist.com,
http://thinkexist.com/quotes/charles_poore/.

[2] "Author Unknown," Religious One Liners, http://www.joe-ks.com/archives_feb2007/Religious_One_Liners.htm.

[3] "Author Unknown," Talk Jesus, http://www.talkjesus.com/lounge/6828-will-god-will-never-take-you.html.

[4] "Ralph Waldo Emerson quotes," About.com:Quotations,
http://quotations.about.com/od/stillmorefamouspeople/a/RalphWaldoEmer7.htm.

[5] "Thomas Jefferson quotes," Quoteworld.org, http://www.quoteworld.org/quotes/7147.

[6] "James Agee quotes," Quoteworld.org,
http://www.quoteworld.org/quotes/233.

[7] "Demosthenes quotes," The Quotation Page,
http://www.quotationspage.com/quote/29680.html.

[8] "Vincent T. Lombardi quotes," Quoteworld.org,
http://www.quoteworld.org/quotes/8402.

[9] "Bernard Edmond quotes," Quoteworld.org,
http://www.quoteworld.org/quotes/4004.

[10] "Vincent T. Lombardi quotes," Quoteworld.org,
http://www.quoteworld.org/quotes/8403.

[11] "Scott Reed quotes," Quoteland.com,
http://www.quoteland.com/author.asp?AUTHOR_ID=621.

[12] "Napoleon Hill quotes," BrainyQuote,
http://www.brainyquote.com/quotes/authors/n/napoleon_hill.html.

[13] "George Bernard Shaw quotes," QuoteDB,
http://www.quotedb.com/quotes/932.

[14] "Abraham Lincoln quotes," quoteworld.org,
http://www.quoteworld.prg/quotes/10282.

[15] "Claude M. Bristol quotes," Thinkexist.com,
http://thinkexist.com/quotes/claude_m_bristol/.

[16] "Elbert Hubbard quotes," QuotationsBook,
http://quotationsbook.com/quote/26725/.

[17] "Dale Carnegie quotes," BrainyQuote,
http://www.brainyquote.com/quotes/authors/d/dale_carnegie.html.

[18] "John McDonald quotes," QuotationsBook,
http://quotationsbook.com/quote/10618/.

[19] "Eric Hoffer quotes," BrainyQuote,
http://www.brainyquote.com/quotes/authors/e/eric_hoffer.html.

[20] "Leo Buscaglia quotes," Hungrybear Blog, ScrapSayings, Love and

Marriage, http://scrapsayings.com/say-love.htm.

[21] "Michael Korda quotes," Thinkexist.com, http://thinkexist.com/quotes/michael_korda/.

[22] ".Whitney. Griswold quotes," Eugene C. Gerhart, Quote It Completely (Buffalo, New York: Wm.S.Hein Publishing, 1998), P.960.

[23] "John D. Rockefeller quotes," the painter's key, http://quote.robertgenn.com/getquotes.php?catid=1.

[24] "Henry Ward Beecher quotes," BrainyQuote, http://www.brainyquote.com/quotes/authors/h/henry_ward_beesher.html.

[25] "Author Unknown, " BellaOnline: The Voice of Women, http://www.bellaonline.com/articles/art41795.asp.

[26] Ibid.

[27] Ibid.

[28] Ibid.

[29] Ibid.

[30] "Tyron Edwards quotes," Thinkexist.com, http://thinkexist.com/quotes/with/keyword/dagger/.

[31] Ibid.

[32] "Albert Pine quotes," Thinkexist.com, http://thinkexist.com/quotes/albert_pine/.

[33] "John Wanamaker quotes," Quote Lady's Quotes, http://www.quotelady.com/subjects/thankfulness.html.

[34] "Pearl Bailey quotes," BrainyQuote, http://www.brainyquote.com/quotes/authors/p/pearl_bailey.html.

[35] "Napoleon Hill quotes," BrainyQuote, http://www.brainyquote.com/quotes/authors/n/napoleon_hill.html.

[36] ".Andy Rooney quotes," My Favorite Ezines, http://www.myfavoriteezines.com/ezinedirectory/quotes-about-aging-elderly.html.

[37] August T. Jaccaci and Susan B. Gault, 2000, CEO – Chief Evolutionary Officer (Woburn, MA, .Butterworth & Heinemann, 1999).

[38] "Andy Rooney Quotes," wowzone, http://www.wowzone.com/rooney.html.

[39] "Peter 3:4," Beauty & Being Beautiful Christian Advice, http://www.christianadvice.net/about_beauty.htm.

[40] "George MacDonald quotes," WorldofQuotes.com, http://www.worldofquotes.com/topic/Help/1/index.html.

[41] "Peter Nivio Zarlenga quotes," Quoteland.com, http://www.quoteland.com/author.asp?AUTHOR_ID=636.

[42] "Francois De La Rochefoucauld quotes," BrainyQuote, http://www.brainyquote.com/quotes/authors/f/framcois_de_la_rochefouca.html.

[43] "Andy Rooney quote," goodreads,
http://www.goodreads.com/quotes/show/132234.
[44] "Josh Billings quotes," Happen-quotes, http://happenstance-music.com/quotes-all.asp.
[45] "Alexander Graham Bell quotes," Wynn Davis, The Best of Success
(Lombard, Illinois: Successories Publishing, 1992), P.70.
[46] "Booker T. Washington quotes," QuoteDB,
http://quotedb.com/authors/booker-t-washington.
[47] "Ralph Waldo Emerson quotes," PBBA Atlantic Inc.,
http://www.pbbaatlantic.com/Default.asp?Page=380.
[48] "Richard Bach quotes," BrainyQuote,
http://www.brainyquote.com/quotes/authors/r/richard_bach.html.
[49] "Ben Stein quotes," Thinkexist.com,
http://thinkexist.com/quotes/ben_stein/.
[50] "Author Unknown," QuotationsBook,
http://quotationsbook.com/quote/27210/.
[51] "George Bernard Shaw quotes," BrainyQuote,
http://www.brainyquote.com/quotes/authors/g/george_bernard_shaw.html.
[52] "B.C. Forbes quotes," BrainyQuote,
http://www.brainyquote.com/quotes/authors/b/b_c_forbes.html.
[53] "Jack Yougblood quotes," BrainyQuote,
http://www.brainyquote.com/quotes/authors/j/jack_youngblood.html.
[54] "John Norley quotes," World of Quotes.com,
http://www.worldofquotes.com/author/John-Norley/i/index.html.
[55] "Josh Billings quotes," BrainyQuote,
http://www.brainyquote.com/quotes/quotes/j/joshbillin161323.html.
[56] Mac Lucado, Six Hours One Friday: Living In The Power Of The
Cross (Nashville, Tennessee, Thomas Nelson Inc. 1989 & 2004). P.43.
[57] "Thomas Carlyle quotes," BrainyQuote,
http://www.brainyquote/quotes/authors/t/thomas_carlyle.html.
[58] "Don Herold quotes," World of Quotes.com,
http://www.worldofquotes/topic/Morality/i/index.html.
[59] "Dwight D. Moody quotes," Bob Kelly, Worth Reading (Grand Rapids,
Michigan: Kregel Publications, 2003).
[60] "Louisa May Alcott quotes," About.com, (Women's History),
http://womenshistory.about.com/cs/quotes/a/qu_lm_alcott.html.
[61] "Jane Ellice Hopkins quotes," Said What,
http://www.saidwhat.com/quotes/favourite/jane_ellice_hopkins.
[62] "Ben Stein quotes," Wynn Davis, The Best of Success (Lombard,
Illinois: Successories Publishing, 1992), P.58.
[63] "Francis Bacon quotes," BrainyQuote,
http://www.brainyquote.com/quotes/authors/f/francis_bacon.html.

[64] "Thomas Moore quotes," Empyrean Friendship Quotes, http://www.empyrean.ca/words/quotes/friends.html.

[65] "Patricia Covalt Ph.D, What Smart Couples Know (New York, NY: Amacom, August, 2007) P.44.

[66] "David Starr Jordan quotes," Thinkexist.com, http://www.thinkexist.com/quotation/wisdom_is_knowing_what_to_do_n ext-skill_is/253363.html.

[67] "Martha Washington quotes," The Quotations Page, http://www.quotationspage.com/quote/Martha_Washington/.

[68] "William James quotes," BrainyQuote, http://www.brainyquote.com/quotes/quotes/w/williamjam163783.html.

[69] "Joseph Marmion quotes," Christianbook.com, http://www.christianbook.com/Christian/Book/product?item_no=722100 &event=cfn.

[70] "Marie Curie quotes," The Quotations Page, http://www.quotationspage.com/quote/34023.html.

[71] "Robert Schuller quotes," fusioncoaching! http://www.fusioncoaching.net/quotes.asp.

[72] "Ben Stein quotes," refdeask.com, http://www.refdesk.com/nov01td.html.

[73] "George Bernard Shaw quotes," Sententiae.org, http://www.sententiae.org/node/67317.

[74] "Norman Dowty quotes," xanga (jmejo327 weblog), http://www.weblog.xanga.com/jmejo327/616206831/item.html?page=1& jump=1373497756&leftcmt=1#1373497756.

[75] "Jose Bergamin quotes," BrainyQuote, http://www,brainyquote.com/quotes/authors/j/jose_bergamin.html.

[76] "Clarence Smithson quotes," My Favorite Ezines, http://www.myfavoriteezines.com/ezinedirectory/quotes-about-faith.html.

[77] "Doris Leasing quotes," quoteworld.org, http://www.quoteworld.org/quotes/8217.

[78] "Daniel H. Burnham quotes," WorldofQuotes.com, http://www.worldofquotes.com/author/Daniel-H-Burnham/1/index.html.

[79] "Jean Paul Satre quotes," WorldofQuotes.com, http://www.worldofquotes.com/topic/Freedom/1/index.html.

[80] "Ralph Waldo Emerson quotes," The Quote Garden, http://www.quotegarden.com/graduation.html.

[81] "Alan Alda quotes," flickr, http://www.flickr.com/photo/journey/tonowhere/190154806/.

[82] "Seneca quotes," HighBeam Research, http://www.highbeam.com/doc/1G1-177290627.html.

[83] "George Patton quotes," QuoteDB,

http://www.quotedb.com/quotes/2092.

[84] "William Penn quotes," BrainyQuote,
http://www.brainyquote.com/quotes/authors/w/william_penn.html.

[85] "William Jennings quotes," quoteworld.org,
http://www.quoteworld.org/quotes/2011.

[86] "Louis Pasteur quotes," QuoteDB,
http://www.quotedb.com/quotes/2195.

[87] "John Ruskin quotes," BrainyQuote,
http://www.brainyquote.com/quotes/quotes/j/johnruskin135097.html.

[88] "George Bernard Shaw quotes," The Quotations Page,
http://www.quotationspage.com/quotes/George_Bernard_Shaw/31.

[89] "English Proverb," PROVERBS AND ENGLISH SAYINGS,
http://www.english-sayings.com/the-hand-that-gives-gathers/4638.

[90] "Bob Richards quotes," BrainyQuote,
http://www.braintquote.com/quotes/authors/b/bob_richards.html.

[91] "Ralph Waldo Emerson quotes," The Quotations Page,
http://www.quotationspage.com/quote/2070.html.

[92] "Dr. Albert Schweitzer quotes," The Quotations Page,
http://www.quotationspage.com/quote/4120.html.

[93] "Author Unknown," The Positivity Blog,
http://www.positivityblog.com/indexphp/2007/04/30/20-inpirational -
quotes-on-happiness/.

[94] "Arnold Toynbee quotes," Thinkexist.com.
http://thinkexist.com/quotes/arnold_toynbee/.

[95] "Flora Edwards quotes," Thinkexist.com.
http://thinkexist.com/quotes/flora_edwards/.

[96] "George Santayana quotes," The Quotations Page,
http://www.quotationspage.com/quotes/George_Santayana.

[97] "Horace quotes," The Quotations Page,
http://www.quotationspage.com/quotes/2954.html.

[98] "Rober J. Mckain quotes," Thinkexist.com.
http://thinkexist.com/quotes/robert_j_mckain/.

[99] "Dwight L. Moody quotes," What Quote,
http://www.whatquote.com/quotes/Dwight_L_Moody/14241-Faith-
makes-all-thin.html.

[100] "Phillips Brooks quotes," Wikiquote,
http://en.wikiquote.org/wiki/Phillips_Brooks.

[101] "Marcus Aurelius quotes," BrainyQuote,
http://www.brainyquote.com/quotes/quoyes/m/marcusaure10790.html.

[102] "Confucius quotes," Thinkexist.com,
http://thinkexist.com/quotations/study_without_reflection_is_a_waste_of
_time/170664.html.

[103] "Paul G. Thomas quotes," DictionaryQuotes,
http://www.dictionaryquotes.com/authorquotations/2873/Paul_G_Thoma
s.php.
[104] "James Allen quotes," BrainyQuote,
http://www.brainyquote.com/quotes/authors/j/james_allen.html.
[105] "Eleanor Roosevelt quotes," Wynn Davis, The Best of Success
(Lombard, Illinois: Successories Publishing, 1992), P.129.
[106] "Albert Einstein quotes," QuotationsBook,
http://quotationsbook.com/quote/19649/.
[107] "Thomas Merton quotes," Thinkexist.com,
http://thinkexist.com/quotes/thomas_merton/.
[108] "Ambrose Bierce quotes, BrainyQuote,
http://www.brainyquote.com/quotes/authors/a/ambrose_bierce.html.
[109] "Bernard M. Baruch quotes," Famous Inspirational Quotes,
http://www.inspirationalquotes4u.com/baruchquotes/index.html.
[110] "James A. Michener quotes," BrainyQuote,
http://www.brainyquote.com/quotes/authors/j/james_a_michener.html.
[111] "H. Stanley Judd quotes," BrainyQuote,
http://www.brainyquote.com/quotes/authors/h/h_stanley_judd.html.
[112] "Robert Louis Stevenson quotes," BrainyQuote,
http://www.brainyquote.com/quotes/authors/r/robert_louis_stevenson.htm
l.
[113] "Thomas Carlyle quotes," BrainyQuote,
http://www.brainyquote.com/quotes/authors/t/thomascarl118220.html.
[114] "Washington Irving quotes," GIGA Quotes, http://www.giga-
usa.com/quotes/authors/washington_irving_a001.html.
[115] "Ralph Waldo Emerson quotes," Quotes and Poem.com,
http://www.quotesandpoem.com/quotes/showquotes/subject/Perseverance
/4923.
[116] "Orison Swett Marden quotes," BrainyQuote,
http://www.brainyquote.com/quotes/authors/o/orison_swett_marden.html.
[117] "Libbie Fudium quotes," QuoteMountain.com,
http://quotemountain.org/sayings/scrapbook_sayings/.
[118] "Albert Camus quotes," Allgreat Quotes,
http://www.allgreatquotes.com/friendship_quotes12.html.
[119] "C. S. Lewis quotes," Thinkexist.com,
http:///www.thinkexist.com/every_day_in_a_life_fills_the_whole_life_wi
th/345885.html.
[120] "Gloria Gaither quotes," Reflections of Moi blog,
http://www.reflectionsofmoiblogspot.com/2007/11/there_is_smothing_in
_every_season_in.html.
[121] "Ralph Waldo Trine quotes," Wynn Davis, The Best of Success

(Lombard, Illinois: Successories Publishing, 1992), P.204,

[122] "J.M. Triggs quotes," Carpe Diem Sermon, October 17, 1996, http://biblestudy.churches.net/base/SEIZE.TXT.

[123] "Author Unknown." The Board of Wisdom, http://www.boardofwisdom.com/mailquote.asp?msgid=38056,

[124] "Plutarch quotes," Quotes about God, http://www.wow4u.com/qgod/index.html,

[125] "Author Unknown," Angelfire, http://www.angelfire.com/mi/peachypenguin/quotes/friend.html,

[126] "Arnold Glasow quotes," Thinkexist.com, http://thinkexist.com/quotes/arnold_h._glasgow/3.html.

[127] "Heabar quotes," Redbubble, http://www.redbubble.com/search/gardener%20sunset?&page=3.

[128] "Orison Swett Marden quotes," Wynn Davis, The Best of Success (Lombard, Illinois: Successories Publishing, 1992), P.58,

[129] "Author Unknown," Country Heart Designs, http:/www.countryheartdesigns.com/friendship.html.

[130] "Abraham Lincoln quotes," Quoteworld.org, www://quoteworld.org/quotes/8336.

[131] "Johnny Cash quotes," Words of Inspiration, http://www.public.asu.edu/~cyndee74/inspire.htm,

[132] "Orison Swett Marden quotes," Quote Cosmos, http://www.quotecosmos.com/quotes/8142view.

[133] "Thomas Merton quotes," UBR, Inc., http://www.quotes.ubr.com/quotes-alphabetical/h-quotes/happiness-quotes.aspx.

[134] "James Keller quotes," cybernation.com, cybernation.com/quotationcenter/quoteshow.php?id123.

[135] "Hellen Keller quotes," MANGERS FORUM, http://managersforum.com/Quotes/QuoteDetail.asp?Type=FEAR.

[136] "Eleanor Roosevelt quotes," The Quotation Page, http://quotationspage.com/quote/26369.html.

[137] "William Feathers quotes," BrainyQuote, http://www.brainyquote.com/quotes/authors/w/william_feathers.html,

[138] "Samuel Johnson quotes," The Quotations Page, http://www.quotationspage.com/quotes/Samuel_Johnson,

[139] "Ted W. Engstrom quotes," quotewold.org, http://www.quoteworld.org/authors/ted_w_engstrom,

[140] "Robert G. Ingersoll quotes," QuotationsBook, http://quotationsbook.com/quote/18384/,

[141] "Orison Swett Marden quotes," Thinkexist.com, http://thinkexist.com/quotes/with/keyword/throbbing/,

194

[142] "William Hazlitt quotes," QuotationsBook,
http://quotationsbook.com/quote/10590/,
[143] "Winston Churchill quotes," QuoteDB,
http://www.quotedb.com/quotes/1039,
[144] "David J. Schwartz quotes," QuotationsBook,
http://quotationsbook.com/quote/30047/,
[145] "Henry Drummond quotes," BrainyQuote,
http://www.brainyquoye.com/quotes/authors/h/henry_drummond.html,
[146] "John Wooden quotes," BrainyQuote,
http://www.brainyquote.com/quotes/authors/j/john_wooden.html,
[147] "Tom Flores quotes," WorldofQuotes.com,
http://www.worldofquotes.com/authors/Tom_Flores/1/index.html,
[148] "Mickey Rooney quotes," The Quotation Page,
http://www.quotationspage.com/quote/1627.html,
[149] "Vince Lombardi quotes," Thinkexist.com,
http://thinkexist.com/quotes/vince_lombardi/,
[150] "Robert Kennedy quotes," QuoteDB,
http://www.quotedb.com/quotes/2713,
[151] "L.D. Turner quotes," Lifebook International, Attitudes of
Blessing:Enthusiasm – February 26, 2008,
http://lifebrook.wordpress.com/2008/02/26/attitudes-of-blessing-
enthusiasm/,
[152] "Author Unknown," Slideshare, http://www.slideshare.net/webtel/26-
beautiful-one-liners,
[153] "Bible quotes," Salvation Economist Weblog, February 18, 2009,
http://salvationeconomist.wordpress.com/,
[154] "Lydia Maria Child quotes," About.com,
http://womenshistory.about.com/od/quotes/a/lm_child.htm,
[155] "Mother Teresa quotes," Thinkexist.com,
http://thinkexist.com/quotation/i_am_a_little_pencil_in_the_hand_of_a_
writing_god/215428.html,

www.ingramcontent.com/pod-product-compliance
Lightning Source LLC
Chambersburg PA
CBHW060239050426
42448CB00009B/1520